M.A. REV. JAMES DAVIES

HESIOD AND THEOGNIS

M.A. REV. JAMES DAVIES

HESIOD AND THEOGNIS

ISBN/EAN: 9783741163982

Manufactured in Europe, USA, Canada, Australia, Japa

Cover: Foto ©Andreas Hilbeck / pixelio.de

Manufactured and distributed by brebook publishing software (www.brebook.com)

M.A. REV. JAMES DAVIES

HESIOD AND THEOGNIS

Ancient Classics for English Readers
EDITED BY THE
REV. W. LUCAS COLLINS, M.A.

HESIOD AND THEOGNIS

A SERIES OF
ANCIENT CLASSICS
FOR
ENGLISH READERS.
EDITED BY
REV. W. LUCAS COLLINS.

20 Vols. Small 12mo. Fine cloth. $1.00 each.

NOW COMPLETE, EMBRACING

1. HOMER'S ILIAD.
2. HOMER'S ODYSSEY.
3. HERODOTUS.
4. CÆSAR.
5. VIRGIL.
6. HORACE.
7. ÆSCHYLUS.
8. XENOPHON.
9. CICERO.
10. SOPHOCLES.
11. PLINY.
12. EURIPIDES.
13. JUVENAL.
14. ARISTOPHANES.
15. HESIOD & THEOGNIS.
16. PLAUTUS & TERENCE.
17. TACITUS.
18. LUCIAN.
19. PLATO.
20. GREEK ANTHOLOGY.

The aim of this delightful series of books is to explain, sufficiently for general readers, who these great writers were, and what they wrote; to give, wherever possible, some connected outline of the story which they tell, or the facts which they record, checked by the results of modern investigations; to present some of their most striking passages in approved English translations, and to illustrate them generally from modern writers; to serve, in short, as a popular retrospect of the chief literature of Greece and Rome.

"Each successive issue only adds to our appreciation of the learning and skill with which this admirable enterprise of bringing the best classics within easy reach of English readers is conducted."—*New York Independent.*

"One of the most ingenious and successful literary enterprises of the day."
—*Every Saturday.*

J. B. LIPPINCOTT & CO., Publishers,
715 and 717 Market St., Philadelphia.

HESIOD AND THEOGNIS

BY THE
REV. JAMES DAVIES, M.A.
LATE SCHOLAR OF LINCOLN COLLEGE, OXFORD
TRANSLATOR OF 'BABRIUS'

PHILADELPHIA
J. B. LIPPINCOTT & CO.
1875.

PREFACE.

THE life of Hesiod, remote from towns, and far away up the gulf of time, and his poetry devoid of sensation and excitement in its almost impersonal didacticism, place the writer who deals with them at a disadvantage, as compared with one whose theme is an ancient epic, or a Greek or Roman historian. He lacks, in a great measure, the choice of parallels by aid of which he may abridge the distance between the shadowy past and the living present. He cannot easily persuade himself or his readers to realise, in the inspired rustic of Ascra, "a heart once pregnant with celestial fire," when he reflects how foreign to the wildest dreams of an English ploughman would be the reduction to verse of his rural experiences, or, still more, of his notions about the divine governance of the universe. Yet this is scarcely an excuse for overlooking the possible contemporary of Homer, the poet nearest to him in claims of antiquity, even if we grant that his style is less interesting, and his matter not so attractive. Indeed one argument for including Hesiod in the series of 'Ancient Classics for English Readers' may be found in the fact that nine out of twelve students finish their classical course with but the vaguest acquaintance with his remains. Such, therefore, ought to be as thankful as the unlearned for an idea of what he actually or probably wrote. And it is this which the larger portion of this volume endeavours to supply. The poet's life has been compiled from ancient and modern biographies with a constant eye to the internal evidence of his extant poetry, for which the editions of Paley, Goettling, and Dubner, have been chiefly studied. For illustrative quotation, use has been chiefly made of the English versions of Elton, good for the most part, and, as regards the Theogony, almost Miltonic. For the 'Works and Days,' the little-known version of the Elizabethan George Chapman—a biographical rarity made accessible by Mr Hooper's edition in J. R. Smith's Library of Old Authors has been here and there pressed into our service. A parallel or two to Hesiod's 'Shield of Hercules,' from Homer's Shield of Achilles, belong to an unpublished version by Mr Richard Garnett. But to no student of Hesiod are so many thanks due as to Mr F. A. Paley, whose notes have been of the utmost use, as the most successful attempt to unravel Hesiodic difficulties and incongruities. Whatever difference of opinion may exist upon his views as to the date and authorship of the Homeric epics, there can be none as to the high value of his edition of Hesiod, which may rank with his Æschylus, Euripides, and Propertius.

For the three chapters about Theognis, which complete this volume, the translation and arrangement of Mr John Hookham Frere have been used and followed. In some instances, where Gaisford's text seemed to discourage freedom of paraphrase, the editor has fallen back upon his own more literal versions. On the whole, however, the debt of Theognis to Mr Hookham Frere, for acting as his exponent to English readers, cannot be over-estimated; and we tender our thanks to his literary executors for permission to avail ourselves of his acute and lively versions. These are marked F. Those of Elton and Chapman in Hesiod are designated by the letters E and C respectively, and the editor's alternative versions by the letter D affixed to them.

CONTENTS.

HESIOD.

		PAGE
CHAP. I. THE LIFE OF HESIOD,	. . . .	1
" II. THE WORKS AND DAYS,	. . .	21
" III. HESIOD'S PROVERBIAL PHILOSOPHY,	. .	59
" IV. THE THEOGONY,	. . . .	79
" V. THE SHIELD OF HERCULES,	. . .	95
" VI. IMITATORS OF HESIOD,	. .	111

THEOGNIS.

CHAP. I. THEOGNIS IN YOUTH AND PROSPERITY,	.	129
" II. THEOGNIS IN OPPOSITION,	. . .	141
" III. THEOGNIS IN EXILE,	. . . .	154

HESIOD.

CHAPTER I.

THE LIFE OF HESIOD.

Of materials for a biography of the father of didactic poetry there is, as might be expected, far less scarcity than is felt in the case of the founder of epic. Classed as contemporaries by Herodotus, Homer and Hesiod represent two schools of authorship—the former the objective and impersonal, wherein the mover of the puppets that fill his stage is himself invisible; the latter the subjective and personal, which communicates to reader and listener, through the medium of its verse, the private thoughts and circumstances of the individual author. Homer, behind the scenes, sets the battles of the Iliad in array, or carries the reader with his hero through the voyages and adventures of the Odyssey. Hesiod, with all the *naïveté* of reality, sets himself in the foreground, and lets us into confidences about his family matters—his hopes and fears, his aims and discouragements, the earnests of his success and the obstacles to it. But notwithstanding the explicitness natural to his school of composition, he has failed to leave any record of the date of his life and poems. For an approximation to this the chief authority is Herodotus, who, in discussing the Hellenic theogonies, gives it as his opinion that "Hesiod and Homer lived not more than four hundred years before" his era, and places, it will be observed, the didactic poet first in order of the two. This would correspond with the testimony of the Parian marble which makes Hesiod Homer's senior by about thirty years; and Ephorus, the historian of the poet's fatherland, maintained, amongst others, the higher antiquity of Hesiod. There was undoubtedly a counter theory, referred to Xenophanes, the Eleatic philosopher, which placed Hesiod later than Homer; but the problem is incapable of decisive solution, and the key to it has to be sought, if anywhere, in the internal evidence of the poems themselves, as to "the state of manners, customs, arts, and political government familiar to the respective authors." Tradition certainly conspires to affix a common date to these pre-eminent stars of Hellenic poetry, by clinging to a fabled contest for the prize of their mutual art; and, so far as it is of any worth, corroborates the consistent belief of the ancients, that Hesiod flourished at least nine centuries before Christ. As to his parentage, although the names of his father and mother have not been preserved, there is internal evidence of the most trustworthy kind. In his 'Works and Days' the poet tells us that his father migrated across the Ægean

from Cyme in Æolia, urged by narrowness of means
and a desire to better his fortunes by a recurrence to
the source and fountain-head of his race; for he sailed
to Bœotia, the mother-country of the Æolian colonies.
There he probably gave up his seafaring life, taking to
agriculture instead; and there—unless, as some have
surmised without much warranty, his elder son,
Hesiod, was born before his migration—he begat two
sons, Hesiod, and a younger brother, Perses, whose
personality is too abundantly avouched by Hesiod to
be any subject of question. Though not himself a
bard, the father must have carried to Bœotia lively
and personal reminiscences and souvenirs of the heroic
poetry for which the Æolic coast of Asia Minor was
then establishing a fame; and his own traditions, together with the intercourse between the mother and
daughter countries, cannot but have nursed a taste for
the muse in Hesiod, which developed itself in a distinct and independent vein, and was neither an offset
of the Homeric stock, nor indebted to the Homeric
poems for aught beyond the countenance afforded by
parity of pursuits. The account given by Hesiod
of his father's migration deserves citation, and may
be conveniently given in the words of Elton's translation of the 'Works and Days:'—

"O witless Perses, thus for honest gain,
Thus did our mutual father plough the main.
Erst from Æolian Cyme's distant shore
Hither in sable ship his course he bore;
Through the wide seas his venturous way he took,
No revenues, not prosperous ease forsook.

His wandering course from poverty began,
The visitation sent from Heaven to man.
In Ascra's wretched hamlet, at the feet
Of Helicon, he fixed his humble seat:
Ungenial clime—in wintry cold severe
And summer heat, and joyless through the year."
—E. 883-894.

An unpromising field, at first sight, for the growth of poesy; but, if the locality is studied, no unmeet "nurse," in its associations and surroundings, "for a poetic child." Near the base of Helicon, the gentler of the twin mountain-brethren towering above the chain that circles Bœotia, Ascra was within easy reach of the grotto of the Libethrian nymphs, and almost close to the spring of Aganippe, and the source of the memory-haunted Permessus. The fountain of Hippocrene was further to the south; but it was near this fountain that the inhabitants of Helicon showed to Pausanias a very ancient copy of the 'Works and Days' of the bard, whose name is inseparably associated with the neighbourhood. Modern travellers describe the locality in glowing colours. "The dales and slopes of Helicon," says the Bishop of Lincoln, in his 'Greece, Pictorial, Descriptive, and Historical.'* "are clothed with groves of olive, walnut, and almond trees; clusters of ilex and arbutus deck its higher plains, and the oleander and myrtle fringe the banks of the numerous rills that gush from the soil, and stream in shining cascades down its declivities into the plain between it and the Copaic Lake. On Helicon," he adds, "according to the ancient belief, no noxious

* P. 253, 254.

herb was found. Here also the first narcissus bloomed. The ground is luxuriantly decked with flowers, which diffuse a delightful fragrance. It resounds with the industrious murmur of bees, and with the music of pastoral flutes, and the noise of waterfalls." The solution of the apparent discrepancy between the ancient settler's account of Ascra and its climate, and that of the modern traveller, is probably to be found in the leaning of the poet Hesiod's mind towards the land which his father had quitted, and which was then more congenial to the growth of poetry—a leaning which may have been enhanced and intensified by disgust at the injustice done to him, as we shall presently see, by the Bœotian law-tribunals. It is, indeed, conceivable that, at certain seasons, Ascra may have been swept by fierce blasts, and have deserved the character given it in the above verses; but the key to its general depreciation at all seasons is more likely to be hid under strong personal prejudice than found in an actual disparity between the ancient and the modern climate. At any rate, it is manifest, from Hesiod's own showing, that the home of his father's settlement had sufficient inducements for him to make it his own likewise; though from the fact that the people of Orchomenus possessed his relics, that Bœotian town may dispute the honour of his birth and residence with Ascra. The latter place, without controversy, is entitled to be the witness of the most momentous incident of his poetic history—to wit, the apparition of the Muses, as he fed his father's flock beside the divine Helicon, when, after one of those night-dances in which

> "They went
> To lead the mazy measure, breathing grace
> Enkindling love, and glance their quivering feet,"—

they accosted the favoured rustic with their heavenly speech, gave him commission to be the bard of didactic, as Homer was of epic, poetry, and in token of such a function invested him with a staff of bay, symbolic of poetry and song. Hesiod's own account of this vision in the opening of his 'Theogony' is as follows:—

> "They to Hesiod erst
> Have taught their stately song, the whilst his flocks
> He fed beneath all-sacred Helicon.
> Thus first those goddesses their heavenly speech
> Addressed, the Olympian Muses born from Jove:
> 'Night-watching shepherds! beings of reproach!
> Ye grosser natures, hear! We know to speak
> Full many a fiction false, yet seeming true,
> Or utter at our will the things of truth.'
> So said they, daughters of the mighty Jove,
> All eloquent, and gave into mine hand,
> Wondrous! a verdant rod, a laurel branch,
> Of bloom unwithering, and a voice imbreathed
> Divine, that I might utter forth in song
> The future and the past, and bade me sing
> The blessed race existing evermore,
> And first and last resound the Muses' praise."
> —E. 33-48.

The details of this interview, as above recorded, are replete with interest—centred, indeed, in the poet himself, but in some degree also attaching to his reputed works. If the verses are genuine—and that the ancients so accounted them is plain from two allusions of Ovid *—they show that with a faith quite in keeping with his simple, serious, superstitious character, he took this night-vision for no idle dream fabric, but a definite call to devote himself to the poetry of truth, and the errand of making song subserve the propagation of religion and moral instruction. The "fictions seeming true"—in other words, the heroic poetry so popular in the land of his father's birth—Hesiod considers himself enjoined to forsake for a graver strain— "the things of truth"—which the Muses declare have been hitherto regarded by mortals as not included in their gift of inspiration. He takes their commission to be prophet and poet of this phase of minstrelsy, embracing, it appears, the past and future, and including his theogonic and ethical poetry. And while the language of the Muses thus defines the poet's aim, when awakened from a rude shepherd-life to the devout service of inspired song, it implies, rather than asserts, a censure of the kinds of poetry which admit of an easier and freer range of fancy. For himself, this supernatural interview formed the starting-point of a path clear to be tracked; and that he accepted his commission as Heaven-appointed is seen in the gratitude which, as we learn from his 'Works and Days,' he evinced by dedicating to the maids of Helicon,

"Where first their tuneful inspiration flowed,"

an *eared tripod*, won in a contest of song at funeral games in Euboea. In the same passage (E. 915-922)

* Fasti, vi. 13; Art of Love, i. 27.

Hesiod testifies to the gravity of his poetic trust by averring that he speaks "the mind of ægis-bearing Jove, whose daughters, the Muses, have taught him the divine song." Pausanias (IX. xxxi. 3) records the existence of this tripod at Helicon in his own day.

But though he took his call as divine, there is no reason to think that Hesiod depended solely on this gift of inspiration for a name and place among poets. His father's antecedents suggest the literary culture which he may well have imbibed from his birthplace in Æolia. His own traditions and surroundings in the mother-country—so near the very Olympus which was the seat of the old Pierian minstrels, whatever it may have been of the fabled gods—so fed by local influences and local cultivation of music and poetry—may have predisposed him to the life and functions of a poet; but there is a distinctly practical tone about all his poetry, which shows that he was indebted to his own pains and thought, his own observation and retentiveness, for the gift which he brought, in his measure, to perfection. A life afield conduced to mould him into the poet of the 'Works and Days,'—a sort of Bœotian 'Shepherd's Calendar,' interwoven with episodes of fable, allegory, and personal history. The nearness of his native hills, as well as the traditions of elder bards, conspired to impel him to the task of shaping a theogony. And both aims are so congenial and compatible, that *prima facie* likelihood will always support the theory of one and the same authorship for both poems against the *separatists*,* who can no more

* The ancient critics who believed in the separate authorship

brook an individual Hesiod than an individual Homer.
But be this as it may, the glimpses which the poet
gives of himself, in the more autobiographical of his
reputed works, present the picture of a not very loco-
motive sage, shrewd, practical, and observant within
his range of observation, apt to learn, and apt also to
teach, storing up life's everyday lessons as they strike
him, and drawing for his poetry upon a well-filled bank
of homely truth and experience. He gives the distinct
idea of one who, having a gift and believing in a commission, sets himself to illustrate his own sentiment,
that "in front of excellence the gods have placed
exertion ;" and whilst in the 'Works and Days' it is
obvious that his aim and drift are the improvement of
his fellow-men by a true detail of his experiences in
practical agriculture, in the 'Theogony' he commands
our respect and reverence for the pains and research
by which he has worked into a system, and this too
for the benefit and instruction of his fellows, the
floating legends of the gods and goddesses and their
offspring, which till his day must have been a chaotic
congeries. On works akin to these two main and
extant poems we may conceive him to have spent
that part of his mature life which was not given up
to husbandry. Travelling he must have disliked—at
any rate, if it involved sea-voyages. His lists of
rivers in the 'Theogony' are curiously defective where
it might have been supposed they would be fullest—as
regards Hellas generally ; whereas he gives many names

of the Iliad and Odyssey were so called, as separating what
by the voice of previous tradition had been made one.

of Asiatic rivers, and even mentions the Nile and the Phasis, neither of which occur in Homer. But this would seem to have been a hearsay knowledge of geography, for he distinctly declares his experience of his father's quondam calling to be limited to a single passage to Euboea from the mainland; and as he is less full when he should enumerate Greek rivers, the reasonable supposition is that he was no traveller, and, depending on tradition, was most correct and communicative touching those streams of which he had heard most in childhood. The one voyage to which he owned was made with a view to the musical contest at Chalcis above alluded to; and it is surely not without a touch of quiet humour that this sailor's son owns himself a landlubber in the following verses addressed to his ne'er-do-well brother:—

"If thy rash thought on merchandise be placed,
Lest debts ensnare or woeful hunger waste,
Learn now the courses of the roaring sea,
Though ships and voyages are strange to me.
Ne'er o'er the sea's broad way my course I bore,
Save once from Aulis to the Euboean shore;
From Aulis, where the mighty Argive host,
The winds awaiting, lingered on the coast,
From sacred Greece assembled to destroy
The guilty walls of beauty-blooming Troy."
— 'Works and Days,' E. 901-910.

This, the poet goes on to say, is all he knows practically about navigation, and truly it is little enough; for it is no exaggeration, but a simple fact, that the strait which constituted Hesiod's sole experience of a

sea voyage was no more than a stretch of forty yards—
a span compared with which the Menai Strait, or the
Thames at any of the metropolitan bridges, would be a
serious business. Emile Burnouf might literally call
the Euripus " le canal Eubéen." In the days of Thucy-
dides a bridge had been thrown across it.

But experimental knowledge was reckoned super-
fluous by one who could rest in the knowledge he
possessed of the mind of Jove, and in the commission
he held from his daughters,—who, according to his belief, taught him navigation, astronomy, and the rest of
the curriculum, when they made him an interpreter of
the divine will, and a " vates " in a double sense,—to
dictate a series of precepts concerning the time for
voyaging and the time for staying ashore. Besides, in
the poet's eye seafaring was a necessity of degenerate
times. In the golden age none were merchants.—
(' Works and Days,' 236.)

Yet the even flow of the poet's rural life was not
without its occasional and chronic disturbances and
storms. The younger brother, to whom allusion has
been made more than once, and whom he generally
addresses as " simple, foolish, good-for-nought Perses,"
had, it seems, come in for a share of the considerable
property which Hesiod's father had got together, after
he exchanged navigation and merchandise for agricultural pursuits. The settlement of the shares in this
inheritance lay with the kings, who in primitive ages
exercised in Bœotia, as elsewhere, the function of judges,
and, according to Hesiod's account, were not superior
to bribery and corruption. Perses found means to

purchase their award to him of the better half of the patrimony, and, after this fraud, dissipated his ill-gotten wealth in luxury and extravagance, a favourite mode of spending his time being that of frequenting the law-tribunals, as nowadays the idletons of a town or district may be known by their lounging about the petty sessional courts when open. Perhaps the taste for litigation thus fostered furnished him with the idea of repairing his diminished fortunes by again proceeding against his brother, and hence Hesiod's invectives against the unscrupulousness of the claimant, and of the judges, who were the instruments of his rapacity. It is not distinctly stated what was the issue of this second suit, which aimed at stripping Hesiod of that smaller portion which had already been assigned to him: perhaps it was an open sore, under the influence of which he wrote his 'Works and Days,'— a persuasive to honest labour as contrasted with the idleness which is fertile in expedients for living at the expense of others—a picture from life of the active farmer, and, as a foil to him, of the idle lounger. Here is a sample of it :—

"Small care be his of wrangling and debate,
 For whose ungathered food the garners wait;
 Who wants within the summer's plenty stored,
 Earth's kindly fruits, and Ceres' yearly hoard:
 With these replenished, at the brawling bar
 For other's wealth go instigate the war:
 But this thou may'st no more; let justice guide,
 Best boon of heaven, and future strife decide.
 Not so we shared the patrimonial land,
 When greedy pillage filled thy grasping hand;

The bribe-devouring judges, smoothed by thee,
The sentence willed, and stamped the false decree:
O fools and blind! to whose misguided soul
Unknown how far the half exceeds the whole,
Unknown the good that healthful mallows yield,
And asphodel, the dainties of the field."
—E. 44-58.

The gnomic character of the last four lines must not blind the reader to the fact that they have a personal reference to the poet and his brother, and represent the anxiety of the former that the latter should adopt, though late, his own life-conviction, and act out the truth that a dinner of herbs with a clear conscience is preferable to the luxuries of plenty purchased by fraud. Consistent with this desire is the unselfish tone in which he constantly recurs to the subject throughout the 'Works and Days,' and that not so much as if he sought to work this change in his brother for peace and quietness to himself, as for a real interest in that brother's amendment—we do not learn with what success. Perhaps, as has been surmised, Perses had a wife who kept him up to his extravagant ways, and to the ready resource of recouping his failing treasure by endeavouring to levy a fresh tax upon Hesiod. Such a surmise might well account for the poet's curious misogynic crotchets. Low as is the value set upon a " help-meet " by Simonides, Archilochus, Bacchylides, and, later still, by Euripides, one might have expected better words in favour of marriage from one whose lost works included a catalogue of celebrated women of old, than the railing tone which accompanies his account of the myth of Pandora, the association of woman with unmixed evil in that legend, and the more practical advice to his brother in a later part of his 'Works and Days,' where he bids him shun the wiles of a woman "dressed out behind" (crinolines and dress-improvers being, it would seem, not by any means modern inventions), and un-paringly lashes the whole sex in the style of the verses we quote :—

"Let no fair woman robed in loose array,
 That speaks the wanton, tempt thy feet astray;
 Who soft demands if thine abode be near,
 And blandly lisps and murmurs in thine ear.
 Thy slippery trust the charmer shall beguile,
 For, lo! the thief is ambushed in her smile."
—E. 511-516.

Indeed, it might be maintained, quite consistently with the internal evidence of Hesiod's poems, that he lived and died a bachelor, seeing perhaps the evil influences of a worthless wife on his brother's establishment and character. It is true that in certain cases (which probably should have come more close in the text to those above cited, whereas they have got shifted to a later part of the poem, where they are less to the point) he prescribes general directions about taking a wife, in just the matter-of-fact way a man would who wrote without passion and without experience. The bridegroom was to be not far short of thirty, the bride about nineteen. Possibly in the injunction that the latter should be sought in the ranks of maidenhood, lurked the same aversion to "marrying a widow" which animated the worldly wise father of

Mr Samuel Weller. Anyhow, he would have had the model wife fulfil the requirements of the beautiful Latin epitaph .on a matron, for he prescribes that she should be "simple-minded" and "home-keeping" (though he says nothing about her being a worker in wools), in lines of which, because Elton's version is here needlessly diffuse, we submit a closer rendering of our own :—

"And choose thy wife from those that round thee dwell,
Weighing, lest neighbours jeer, thy choice full well.
Than wife that's good man finds no greater gain,
But feast-frequenting males are simply bane.
Such without fire a stout man's frame consume,
And to crude old age bring his manhood's bloom."
—'Works and Days,' 700-705.

This, we conceive, was Hesiod's advice, as an outsider might give it, to others. For himself, it is probable he reckoned that the establishment would suffice which he elsewhere recommends to the farmer class—an unmarried bailiff, a housekeeper without encumbrances; for a female servant with children, he remarks, in bachelor fashion, is troublesome—and a dog that bites (see 'Works and Days,' 602-604). It is indirectly confirmatory of this view that tradition, which has built up many absurd figments upon the scant data of Hesiod's autobiography, has signally failed to fasten other offspring to his name than the intellectual creations which have kept it in remembrance. This was surely Plato's belief when he wrote the following beautiful sentences in his 'Symposium.'

"Who when he thinks of Homer and Hesiod and other great poets, would not rather have their children than ordinary human ones? Who would not emulate them in the creation of children such as theirs, which have preserved their memory, and given them everlasting glory?" *

So far as the poet's life and character can be approximately guessed from his poems, it would seem to have been temperately and wisely ordered, placid, and for the most part unemotional. That one who so clearly saw the dangers of association with bad women that he shrank from intimacy with good, should have met his death through an intrigue at Œnoe, in Ozolian Locris, with Clymene, the sister of his hosts, is doubtless just as pure a bit of incoherent fiction as that his remains were carried ashore, from out of the ocean into which they had been cast, by the agency of dolphins; or that a faithful dog—no doubt the sharp-toothed specimen we have seen recommended in the 'Works and Days'—traced out the authors of the murder, and brought them to the hands of justice. Some accounts attribute to the poet only a guilty knowledge of the crime of a fellow-lodger; but in either shape the legend is an after-thought, as is also the halting story that Stesichorus, who lived from B.C. 643 to B.C. 560, was the off-spring of this fabled *liaison*. All that can be concluded from trustworthy data for his biography, beyond what has been already noticed, is that in later life he must have exchanged his residence at Ascra for Orchomenus, possibly to be further from the importunities of

* Jowett's transl., i. 525.

Perses, and beyond the atmosphere of unrighteous judges. Pausanias states that Hesiod, like Homer, whether from fortune's spite or natural distaste, enjoyed no intimacy with kings or great people; and this consists with Plutarch's story that the Spartan Cleomenes used to call Hesiod "the poet of the Helots," in contrast with Homer, "the delight of warriors," and with the inference from an expression in the 'Works and Days' that the poet and his father were only resident aliens in Bœotia. In Thespiæ, to which realm he belonged, agriculture was held degrading to a freeman, which helps to account for his being, in his own day, a poet only of the peasantry and the lower classes. Pausanias and Paterculus do but retail tradition; but this suffices to corroborate the impression, derived from the poet's own works, of a calm and contemplative life, unclouded except by the worthlessness of others, and owing no drawbacks to faults or failings of its own. Musing much on the deities whose histories he systematised as best he might, and at whose fanes, notwithstanding all his research and inquiry, he still ignorantly worshipped; regulating his life on plain and homely moral principles, and ever awake to the voice of mythology, which spoke so stirringly to dwellers in his home of Bœotia,—Hesiod lived and died in that mountain-girded region, answerably to the testimony of the epitaph by his countryman Chersias, which Pausanias read on the poet's sepulchre at Orchomenus:—

"Though fertile Ascra gave sweet Hesiod birth,
Yet rest his bones beneath the Minyan earth,

Equestrian land. There, Hellas, sleeps thy pride,
The wisest bard of bards in wisdom tried."
—Pausan., ix. 38, § 4.

The question of Hesiod's literary offspring has been much debated, the 'Works and Days' alone enjoying an undisputed genuineness. But it does not seem that the 'Theogony' was impugned before the time of Pausanias,* who records that Hesiod's Heliconian fellow-citizens recognised only the 'Works and Days.' On the other hand—to say nothing of internal evidence in the 'Theogony'—we have the testimony of Herodotus to Hesiod's authorship; whilst the ancient popular opinion on this subject finds corroboration in Plato's direct allusion to a certain passage of the 'Theogony' as Hesiod's recognised work. Alluding to vv. 116-118 of the 'Theogony,' the philosopher writes in the 'Symposium' (178),—"As Hesiod says,—

'First Chaos came, and then broad-bosomed Earth,
  The everlasting seat of all that is,
  And Love.'

In other words, after Chaos, the Earth and Love, these two came into being." Aristophanes, also, in more than one drama, must be considered to refer to the 'Theogony' and the "Works." Furthermore, it is certain that the Alexandrian critics, to whom scepticism in the matter would have opened a congenial field, never so much as hinted a question concerning the age and authorship of the 'Theogony.' Besides these two works, but one other poem has

ix. 31, § 3.

descended to our day under the name of Hesiod,
unless, indeed, we take as a sample of his 'Eoiæ, or
Catalogue of Heroines,' the fifty-six verses which,
having slipped their cable, have got attached to the
opening of 'The Shield of Hercules.' The 'Shield'
is certainly of questionable merit, date, and authorship,
though a little hesitation would have been wise in
Colonel Mure, before expressing such wholesale con-
demnation and contempt as he heaps upon it.[*] These
three poems, at all events, are what have come down
under the name and style of Hesiod, and are our
specimens of the three classes of poetical composition
which tradition imputes to him:—(1) didactic; (2)
historical and genealogical; (3) short mythical poems.
Under one or other of these heads it is easy to group
the Hesiodic poems, no longer extant, of which notices
are found in ancient authors. Thus the 'Astronomy'
and the 'Maxims of Chiron,' with the 'Ornithoman-
teia, or Book of Augury,' belong to the first class; the
'Eoiæ, or Catalogue of Women,' which is probably
the same poem as the 'Genealogy of Heroes;' the
'Melampodia,' which treated of the renowned prophet, prince, and priest of the Argives, Melampus, and
of his descendants in genealogical sequence; and the
'Æginius,' which gathered round the so-named mythical prince of the Dorians, and friend and ally of
Hercules, many genealogical traditions of the Heraclid
and Dorian races,—will, with the extant 'Theogony,'
represent the second; while the smaller epics of 'The
Marriage of Ceyx,' 'The Descent to Hades of Theseus,'

[*] History of Greek Lit., ii. 424.

and the 'Epithalamium of Peleus and Thetis,' will
keep in countenance the sole extant representative of
the third class, and enhance the possibility that 'The
Shield of Hercules' is at least *Hesiodic*, though it is
safer to put it thus vaguely than to affirm it Hesiod's.
A conveniently wide berth is afforded by the modern
solution, that several imputed works of Hesiod are the
works of a school of authors of which Hesiod was the
name-giving patriarch. The truth in this matter can
only be approximated. Enough, perhaps, is affirmed
when we say that in style, dialect, and flavour of antiquity, the 'Theogony' and the 'Works' are more akin
to each other than to the 'Shield;' while, at the
same time, the last-named poem is of very respectable
age. The two former poems are of the Æolo-Bœotic
type of the ancient epic dialect, while the 'Shield' is
nearer to the Æolo-Asiatic branch of it, used by
Homer. Discrepancies, where they occur, may be set
down to the interpolations of rhapsodists, and to the
accretions incident to passage through the hands of
many different workmen, after the original master.
The style and merits of each work will best be dis-
cussed separately; and we shall give precedence to
Hesiod's most undoubted poem, the 'Works and
Days.'

CHAPTER II.

THE WORKS AND DAYS.

The meaning of the title prefixed to Hesiod's great didactic poem appears to be properly "Farming Operations," "Lucky and Unlucky Days," or, in short, "The Husbandman's Calendar;" but if the ethical scope of it be taken into account, it might, as Colonel Mure has remarked, be not inaptly described as "A Letter of Remonstrance and Advice to a Brother." And inasmuch as its object is to exhort that brother to amend his ways, and take to increasing his substance by agriculture, rather than dreaming of schemes to enhance it by frequenting and corrupting the law-courts, the two descriptions are not inconsistent with each other. It has been imputed as blame to the poem that it hangs loosely together, that its connection is obscure and vague,—in short, that its constituent parts, larger and smaller, are seldom fitly jointed and compacted. But some allowance is surely to be made for occasional tokens of inartistic workmanship in so early a poet, engaged upon a task where he had neither pattern nor master to refer to; and besides

this, a closer study of the whole will prove that the
want of connectedness in the work is more seeming
than real. Didactic poetry, from Hesiod's day until
the present, has ever claimed the privilege of arrang-
ing its hortatory topics pretty much as is most con-
venient, and of enforcing its chief idea, be that what
it may, by arguments and illustrations rather congru-
ous in the main than marshalled in the best order of
their going. But the 'Works and Days' is capable
of tolerably neat division and subdivision. The first
part (vv. 1-383) is ethical rather than didactic,— a set-
ting-forth by contrast, and by the accessory aid of
myth, fable, allegory, and proverb-lore, of the superi-
ority of honest labour to unthrift and idleness, and of
worthy emulation to unworthy strife and envying.
The second part (vv. 384-764) consists of practical
hints and rules as to husbandry, and, in a true didactic
strain, furnishes advice how best to go about that
which was the industrious Bœotian's proper and chief
means of subsistence. It thus follows naturally on
the general exhortation to honest labour which formed
the first part of the poem. The third and last part
is a religious calendar of the months, with remarks
upon the days most lucky or unpropitious for this or
that duty or occupation of rural and nautical life. All
three, however, more or less address Perses as "a sort
of ideal reader," and thus hang together quite sufficiently for didactic coherence; whilst in each of the
two first parts episodic matter helps to relieve the dry
routine of exhortation or precept, and is introduced, as
we shall endeavour to show, with more skill and sys-

tem than would appear to a perfunctory reader. The
first part, as is almost universally agreed by editors
and commentators, begins properly at v. 11, which
in the Greek reads as if it were a correction of the
view held by the author in his 'Theogony,' that
there was but one "Eris," or "Contention," and which is
therefore of some slight weight in the question of unity
of authorship for the two poems. The introductory
ten verses are in all probability nothing more than
a shifting proem, in the shape of an address to Jove
and the Muses, available for the use of the Hesiodian
rhapsodists, in common with divers other like intro-
ductions. According to Pausanias, the Heliconians,
who kept their countryman's great work engraved on
a leaden tablet, knew nothing of these ten verses.
Starting, then, at this point, the poet distinguishes
between two goddesses of strife, the one pernicious
and discord-sowing, the other provocative of honest
enterprise. The elder and nobler of the twain is the
parent of healthy competition, and actuates mechanics
and artists, as well as bards and beggars, between
which last trades it is obvious that the poet traces a
not fortuitous connection:—

> "Beneficent this better envy burns,—
> Thus emulous his wheel the potter turns,
> The smith his anvil beats, the beggar throng
> Industrious ply, the bards contend in song."
> —E. 33-36.

The wandering minstrel and the professional beggar
of the heroic age exercise equally legitimate callings
in Hesiod's view, and the picture which he draws

recalls to us those of the banquet-hall in the Odyssey.
When Antinous rates the swine-herd Eumaeus for
bringing Ulysses disguised as a beggar-man into the
hall of feasting, his grievance is that

> "Of the tribes
> Of vagrants and mean mendicants that prey,
> As kill-joys, at our banquets, we have got
> A concourse ample. Is it nought to thee
> That such as these, here gathering, all the means
> Of thy young master waste?"
> —Odyssey, xvii. 624-628 (Musgrave).

It is probable that the beggar's place was nearer the
threshold than that of Phemius the bard, who had
just before been singing to his harp, or of other inspired minstrels, of whom it is said that

> "These o'er all the world
> At all feasts are made welcome."
> —Odyssey, xvii. 639-641 (Musgrave).

But that he had an assured footing and dole in such
assemblies is plain from Irus's jealousy of a supposed
rival beggar, which results in the boxing-match with
Ulysses in the 18th Book.

To return to Hesiod. The bettermost kind of rivalry
is the goddess to whom he would have Perses give
heed, and not her wrangling sister, who inspires
wrongful dealing, chicanery, and roguish shifts, and
has no fancy for fair-play or healthy emulation. She,
says the poet, has had it too much her own way since
Prometheus stole the fire from heaven, because Zeus,
as a punishment, made labour toilsome, and the idle,

to shirk their inevitable lot, resort to injustice. "If
the gods had not ordained toil, men might stow away
their boat-paddles over the smoke, and there would be
an end to ploughing with mules and oxen:"—

> "But Zeus our food concealed: Prometheus' art
> With fraud illusive had incensed his heart;
> Sore ills to man devised the heavenly sire,
> And hid the shining element of fire.
> Prometheus then, benevolent of soul,
> In hollow reed the spark recovering stole,
> And thus the god beguiled, whose awful gaze
> Serene rejoices in the lightning blaze."
> —E. 67-74.

Till the Titan's offence, toil and sickness and human
ills had been unknown; but after that transgression
they were introduced — as sin into the world through
our mother Eve—by Zeus's "beauteous evil," Pandora.
The Father creates her, and the immortals rival each
other in the gifts that shall make her best adapted for
her work of witchery, and presently send her as a gift
to Epimetheus, the personification of "Unreflection,"
who takes her in spite of the remonstrances of his
elder and more foresighted brother, Prometheus. If,
as has been suggested, we may take the wise Prometheus to represent the poet, and Perses to be implied
in the weaker Epimetheus—and if, too, in Pandora
there is a covert allusion to the foolish wife of Perses,
who encouraged his extravagance, and seems to have
inspired Hesiod with an aversion for her sex—it will
bring home the more closely the pertinence of this
myth to the moral lesson which, in the first part of

the poem, the poet designed to teach. The creation
and equipment of Pandora is one of Hesiod's finest
flights above a commonly-even level:—

> "The Sire who rules the earth and sways the pole
> Had said, and laughter filled his secret soul:
> He bade the crippled god his hest obey,
> And mould with tempering water plastic clay;
> With human nerve and human voice invest
> The limbs elastic, and the breathing breast;
> Fair as the blooming goddesses above,
> A virgin's likeness with the looks of love.
> He bade Minerva teach the skill that sheds
> A thousand colours in the gliding threads;
> He called the magic of love's golden queen
> To breathe around a witchery of mien,
> And eager passion's never-sated flame,
> And cares of dress that prey upon the frame;
> Bade Hermes last endue with craft refined
> Of treacherous manners, and a shameless mind."
> —E. 83-99.

The Olympians almost overdo the bidding of their
chief, calling in other helpers besides those named in
the above extract:—

> "Adored Persuasion and the Graces young,
> Her tapered limbs with golden jewels hung;
> Round her fair brow the lovely-tressèd Hours
> A golden garland twined of spring's purpureal flowers."
> —E. 103-106.

And when the conclave deemed that they had perfected an impersonation of mischief,—

> "The name Pandora to the maid was given,
> For all the gods conferred a gifted grace
> To crown this mischief of the mortal race.

> The sire commands the wingèd herald bear
> The finished nymph, the inextricable snare;
> To Epimetheus was the present brought,
> Prometheus' warning vanished from his thought—
> That he disclaim each offering from the skies,
> And straight restore, lest ill to man should rise.
> But he received, and conscious knew too late
> The invidious gift, and felt the curse of fate."
> —E. 114-124.

How this gift of "woman" was to be the source of prolific evil and sorrow, the poet, it must be confessed, does not very coherently explain. Nothing is said, in the account of her equipment, of any chest or casket sent with her by Zeus, or any other god, as an apparatus for propagating ills. And when in v. 94 of the poem we are brought face to face with the chest and the lid, and Pandora's fatal curiosity, the puzzle is "how they got there." Homer, indeed, glances at two chests, one of good the other of evil gifts, in Jove's heavenly mansion:—

> "Two casks there stand on Zeus' high palace-stair,
> One laden with good gifts, and one with ill:
> To whomso Zeus ordains a mingled share,
> Now in due time with foul he meeteth, now with fair."
> —Conington, Il. xxiv.

And those who hold Hesiod to have lived after Homer, or to have availed himself here and there of the same pre-existent legends, may infer that the poet leaves it to be surmised that Pandora was furnished with the less desirable casket for the express purpose of woe to man. But it is a more likely solution that Prometheus, the embodiment of mythic philanthropy, had imprisoned "human ills" in a chest in the abode of Epimetheus, and this chest was tampered with through the same craving for knowledge which actuated Mother Eve. This account is supported by the authority of Proclus. In Hesiod, the first mention of the chest is simultaneous with the catastrophe—

"The woman's hands an ample casket bear;
She lifts the lid—she scatters ills in air.
Hope sole remained within, nor took her flight,
Beneath the casket's verge concealed from sight.
The unbroken cell with closing lid the maid
Sealed, and the cloud-assembler's voice obeyed.
Issued the rest, in quick dispersion hurled,
And woes innumerous roamed the breathing world;
With ills the land is rife, with ills the sea;
Diseases haunt our frail humanity:
Self-wandering through the noon, the night, they glide
Voiceless—a voice the Power all-wise denied.
Know then this awful truth: it is not given
To elude the wisdom of omniscient Heaven."
—E. 131-144.

It is a beautiful commentary on that part of the legend which represents Hope as lying not at the bottom of the casket, but just beneath the lid which in closing shuts her in, that this did not happen through inadvertence on Pandora's part, but with her connivance, and that of her divine prompter, who, though desirous to punish mankind, represents a partial benefactor to the race. The concluding lines of the last extract recall the reader to the drift of the first part of the poem, by repeating that the moral governance of the universe will not suffer wrong to go unpunished, or allow innocence to succumb to fraud.

And yet, the poet goes on to argue, the times in which he lives are out of joint. Such men as his brother prosper in an age which in wickedness distances its precursors. His lot, he laments, is cast in the fifth age of the world; and here he takes occasion to introduce the episode of the five ages of the world, and of the increase of corruption as each succeeds the other. In this episode, which Mr Paley considers to bear a more than accidental resemblance to the Mosaic writings, the golden age comes first — those happy times under Cronos or Saturn, when there was neither care nor trouble nor labour, but life was a blameless holiday spent in gathering self-sown fruits; and death, unheralded by decay or old age, coming to men even as a sleep, was the very ideal of an Euthanasia:—

"Strangers to ill, they nature's banquets proved,
Rich in earth's fruits, and of the blest beloved,
They sank in death, as opiate slumber stole
Soft o'er the sense, and whelmed the willing soul.
Theirs was each good—the grain-exuberant soil
Poured its full harvest uncompelled by toil:
The virtuous many dwelt in common blest,
And all unenvying shared what all in peace possessed."
—E. 155-162.

It was with sin, in Hesiod's view as in that of the author of the Book of Genesis, that death, deserving the name, came into the world. As for the golden race, when earth in the fulness of time closed upon it, they became dæmons or genii, angelic beings invisibly

moving over the earth—a race of which Homer, indeed,
says nought, but whose functions, shadowed forth in
Hesiod, accord pretty much with the account Diotima
gives of them in the 'Banquet of Plato.'* Here is
Hesiod's account: —

" When on this race the verdant earth had lain,
By Jove's high will they rose a 'genii' train;
Earth-wandering demons they their charge began,
The ministers of good, and guards of man:
Veiled with a mantle of aerial night,
O'er earth's wide space they wing their hovering flight,
Disperse the fertile treasures of the ground,
And bend their all-observant glance around;
To mark the deed unjust, the just approve,
Their kingly office, delegates of Jove."
—E. 163-172.

With this dim forecasting by a heathen of the " ministry of angels " may be compared the poet's reference
further on in the poem to the same invisible agency,
where he uses the argument of the continual oversight
of these thrice ten thousand genii as a dissuasive to
corrupt judgments, such as those which the Bœotian
judges had given in favour of his brother:—

" Invisible the gods are ever nigh,
Pass through the midst, and bend the all-seeing eye;
Who on each other prey, who wrest the right,
Aweless of Heaven's revenge, are open to their sight.
For thrice ten thousand holy demons rove
The nurturing earth, the delegates of Jove;
Hovering they glide to earth's extremest bound,
A cloud aerial veils their forms around—

* Jowett's transl., i. 519.

Guardians of man; their glance alike surveys
The upright judgments and the unrighteous ways."
—E. 331-310.

In the second or silver age began declension and degeneracy. The blessedness of this race consisted in long retention of childhood and its innocence—even up to a hundred years. Manhood attained, it became quarrelsome, irreligious, and ungrateful to the gods—its creators. This generation soon had an end:

"Jove angry hid them straight in earth,
Since to the blessèd deities of heaven
They gave not those respects they should have given.
But when the earth had hid these, like the rest,
They then were called the subterrestrial blest,
And in bliss second, having honours then
Fit for the infernal spirits of powerful men."
—C. 135-142.

In Hesiod's account of this race it is curious to note a correspondence with holy Scripture as to the term of life in primitive man; curious, too, that Jove is not said to have created, but to have laid to sleep, the silver race. It obtained from men, after its demise, the honours of propitiatory sacrifice, and represented the "blessed spirits of the departed," and perhaps the "Manes" of the Latin, without, however, attaining to immortality. A rougher type was that of the brazen age, which the Elizabethan translator Chapman seems right in designating as

"Of wild ash fashioned, stubborn and austere,"—

though another way of translating the words which he

so interprets represents these men of brass as "mighty by reason of their ashen spears." The question is set at rest by the context, in which the arms of this race are actually said to have been of brass. This age was hard and ferocious, and, unlike those preceding it, carnivorous. It perished by mutual slaughter, and found an end most unlike the posthumous honours of the silver race, in an ignominious descent to Hades:

" Their thoughts were bent on violence alone,
The deeds of battle and the dying groan:
Bloody their feasts, by wheaten bread unblest;
Of adamant was each unyielding breast.
Huge, nerved with strength, each hardy giant stands,
And mocks approach with unresisted hands;
Their mansions, implements, and armour shine
In brass—dark iron slept within the mine.
They by each other's hands inglorious fell,
In horrid darkness plunged, the house of hell.
Fierce though they were, their mortal course was run,
Death gloomy seized, and snatched them from the sun."
—E. 193-204.

At this stage Hesiod suspends awhile the downward course of ages and races, and reflecting that, having commemorated the "genii" on earth and the blessed spirits in Hades, he must not overlook the "heroes," a veneration for whom formed an important part of the religion of Hellas, brings the "heroic age"—apparently unmetallic—into a place to which their prowess entitled them, next to the brazen age; and at the same time, contrasting their virtues with the character of their violent predecessors, assigns to them an after-

state nearer to that of the gold and silver races. Of
their lives and acts Hesiod tells us that—

> "These dread battle hastened to their end ;
> Some when the sevenfold gates of Thebes ascend,
> The Cadmian realm, where they with savage might
> Strove for the flocks of Œdipus in fight :
> Some war in navies led to Troy's far shore,
> O'er the great space of sea their course they bore,
> For sake of Helen with the golden hair,
> And death for Helen's sake o'erwhelmed them there."
> — E. 211-218.

Their rest is in the Isles of the Blest, and in

> "A life, a seat, distinct from human kind,
> Beside the deepening whirlpools of the main,
> In those black isles where Cronos holds his reign,
> Apart from heaven's immortals ; calm they share
> A rest un-sullied by the clouds of care.
> And yearly, thrice with sweet luxuriance crowned,
> Springs the ripe harvest from the teeming ground."
> — E. 220-226.

Who does not recognise the same regions beyond
circling ocean, of which Horace long after says in his
sixteenth Epode,—

> "The rich and happy isles,
> Where Ceres year by year crowns all the untilled land with
>   sheaves,
> And the vine with purple clusters droops, unpruned of all
>   her leaves.
>   .   .   .   .
> Nor are the swelling seeds burnt up within the thirsty
>   clods,
> So kindly blends the seasons there the king of all the gods.

For Jupiter, when he with brass the golden age alloyed,
That blissful region set apart by the *good* to be enjoyed."
—Theodore Martin, p. 212.

But with this exception and interval, the ages tend to the worse. Now comes the iron age, corrupt, unrestful, and toilsome; wherein, in strong contrast to the silver age, which enjoyed a hundred years of childhood and youth, premature senility is an index of physical degeneracy:—

"Scarcely they spring into the light of day,
Ere age untimely shows their temples grey."
—E. 237, 238.

With this race, Hesiod goes on to tell us, family ties, the sanctity of oaths, and the plighted faith, are dead letters. Might is right. Lynch-lawyers get the upper hand. All is "violence, oppression, and sword law," and

"Though still the gods a weight of care bestow,
And still some good is mingled with the woe,"

yet, as this iron age, at the transition point of which Hesiod's own lot is cast, shades off into a lower and worse generation, the lowest depth will at length be reached, and baseness, corruption, crooked ways and words, will supplant all nobler impulses,

"Till those fair forms, in snowy raiment bright,
From the broad earth have winged their heavenward flight
Called to th' eternal synod of the skies,
The virgins, Modesty and Justice, rise,
And leave forsaken man to mourn below
The weight of evil and the cureless woe."
—E. 259-264.

Having thus finished his allegory of the five ages, and identified his own generation with the last and worst, it is nowise abrupt or unseasonable in the poet to bring home to the kings and judges of Bœotia their share in the blame of things being as they are, by means of an apologue or fable. Some have said that it ought to be entitled "The Hawk and the Dove," but Hesiod probably had in his mind the legend of Tereus and Philomela; and the epithet attached to the nightingale in v. 268 probably refers to the tincture of green on its dark-coloured throat, with which one of our older ornithologists credits that bird. The fable is as follows, and it represents oppression and violence in their naked repulsiveness. Contrary to the use of later fabulists, the moral is put in the mouth of the hawk, not of the narrator:—

"A stooping hawk, crook-taloned, from the vale
Bore in his pounce a neck-streaked nightingale,
And snatched among the clouds; beneath the stroke
This piteous shrieked, and that imperious spoke:
'Wretch, why these screams! a stronger holds thee now;
Where'er I shape my course a captive thou,
Maugre thy song, must company my way;
I rend my banquet, or I loose my prey.
Senseless is he who dares with power contend;
Defeat, rebuke, despair shall be his end."
—E. 267-276.

From fable the poet passes at once to a more direct appeal. Addressing Perses and the judges, he points out that injustice and overbearing conduct not only crush the poor man, but eventually the rich and powerful fail to stand against its consequences. He pictures the rule of wrong and the rule of right, and forcibly contrasts the effects of each on the prosperity of communities. Here are the results of injustice :—

> "Lo! with crooked judgments runs th' avenger stern
> Of oaths forsworn, and eke the murmuring voice
> Of Justice rudely dragged, where base men lead
> Thro' greed of gain, and olden rights misjudge
> With verdict perverse. She with mist enwrapt
> Follows, lamenting homes and haunts of men,
> To deal out ills to such as drive her forth,
> By custom of wrong judgment, from her seats."—D.

And here, by contrast, are the fruits of righteousness and justice, practised by cities and nations :—

> "Genial peace
> Dwells in their borders, and their youth increase.
> Nor Zeus, whose radiant eyes behold afar,
> Hangs forth in heaven the signs of grievous war.
> Nor scathe nor famine on the righteous prey :
> Earth foodful teems, and banquets crown the day.
> Rich wave their mountain oaks ; the topmost tree
> The rustling acorn fills, its trunk the murmuring bee.
> Burdened with fleece their panting flocks ; *the race
> Of woman soft reflects the father's face :*
> Still flourish they, nor tempt with ships the main;
> The fruits of earth are poured from every plain."
> —E. 303-314.

In the lines italicised the old poet anticipates that criterion of honest wedlock which Horace shapes into the line, " The father's features in his children smile " (Odes, iv. 5-23, Con.); and Catullus into the beautiful wish for Julia and Manlius, that their offspring

> "May strike
> Strangers when the boy they meet
> As his father's counterfeit;
> And his face the index be
> Of his mother's chastity."
> —Epithalam. (Theod. Martin).

After a recurrence, suggested by this train of thought, to the opposite picture, and an appeal to the judges to remember those invisible watchers who evermore support the right and redress the wrong, as well as the intercession of Justice at the throne of Zeus for them that are defrauded and oppressed, the poet for a moment resorts to irony, and, like Job, asks " what profit there is in righteousness, when wrong seems to carry all before it?" But only for a moment. In a short but fine image, Perses is invited to lift up his eyes to the distant seat,—

> " Where virtue dwells on high, the gods before
> Have placed the dew that drops from every pore.
> And at the first to that sublime abode
> Long, steep the ascent, and rough the rugged road.
> But when thy slow steps the rude summit gain,
> Easy the path, and level is the plain."
> —E. 389-394.

He is urged again to rely on his own industry, and encouraged to find in work the antidote to famine, and the favour of bright-crowned Demeter, who can fill his barns with abundance of corn. That which is laid up in your own granary (he is reminded in a series of terse economic maxims, which enforce Hesiod's general exhortation) does not trouble you like that which you borrow, or that which you covet. Honesty is the best policy. Shame is found with poverty born of idleness; whereas a just boldness inspirits him whose wealth is gained by honest work and the favour of Heaven. Some of these adagial maxims will form part of the chapter on "Hesiod's Proverbial Philosophy;" and of the rest it may suffice to say, that the poet has his own quaint forceful way of prescribing the best rules for dealing with friends and neighbours, as to giving and entertaining, and with regard to women, children, and domestics. In most of these maxims the ruling motive appears to be *expediency*. In reference to the fair sex, it is plain that he is on the defensive, and regards them as true representatives of Pandora, with whom the less a man has to do, the less he will be duped, the less hurt will there be to his substance. As old Chapman renders it,

"He that gives
A woman trust doth trust a den of thieves."
— C. 585.

As to family, his view is that "the more children the more cares." * The best thing is to have an only son, to nurse and consolidate the patrimony; and if a man has more, it is to be desired that he should die old, so as to prevent litigation (a personal grievance this) between young heirs. And yet, adds the pious bard, it lies with Zeus to give store of wealth to even a large family; and he seems to imply that where such

* "He that hath a wife and children hath given pledges to fortune."-- BACON.

a family is thrifty there will be the greater aggregate increase of property. Such is the advice, he remarks in concluding the first part of his poem, which he has to offer to any one who desires wealth; to observe these rules and cautions, and to devote himself to the systematic routine of the farming operations, which, to his mind, constitute the highroad to getting rich.

From the very outset of the second part of the 'Works and Days,' a more definite and practical character attaches to Hesiod's precepts touching agriculture. Hitherto his exhortation to his brother had harped on the one string of " work, work ;" and now, as agriculture was the Bœotian's work, he proceeds to prescribe and illustrate the *modus operandi*, and the seasons best adapted for each operation. This is really the didactic portion of Hesiod's Georgics, if we may so call his poem on agriculture; and it is curiously interesting to study, by the light he affords, the theory and practice of *very* old-world farming.

As apparently he was ignorant of any calendar of months by which the time of year might be described, he has recourse to the rising and setting of the stars, whose annual motion was known to him, to indicate the seasons of the year. Thus the husbandman is bidden to begin cutting his corn at the rising of the Pleiads (in May), and his ploughing when they set (in November). They are invisible for forty days and nights, during which time, as he tells us later on, sailing, which with the Bœotian was second in importance to agriculture (inasmuch as it subserved the exportation of his produce), was suspended, and works on the farm came on instead. To quote Elton's version:—

"When Atlas-born the Pleiad stars arise
Before the sun above the dawning skies,
'Tis time to reap; and when they sink below
The morn-illumined west, 'tis time to sow.
Know too, they set, immerged into the sun,
While forty days entire their circle run;
And with the lapse of the revolving year,
When sharpened is the sickle, reappear.
Law of the fields, and known to every swain
Who turns the laboured soil beside the main;
Or who, remote from billowy ocean's gales,
Fills the rich glebe of inland-winding vales."
—E. 525-536.

With Hesiod, therefore, as with us, ploughing and sowing began, for early crops, in late autumn; and to be even with the world around him, and not dependent on his neighbours, a man must (he tells his ne'er-do-well brother) "strip to plough, strip to sow, and strip to reap,"—advice which Virgil has repeated in his first Georgic. He seems to imply, too, in v. 398, that it is a man's own fault if he does not avail himself of the times and the seasons which the Gods have assigned and ordained, and of which the stars are meant to admonish him. If he neglect to do so, he and his wife and children cannot reasonably complain if friends get tired of repeated applications for relief. But suppose the better course of industrious labour resolved upon. The first thing the farmer has to do is to take a house, and get an unmarried female slave, and an ox to plough with, and then the farming im-

plements suited to his land. It will never do to be
always borrowing, and so waiting till others can lend,
and the season has glided away. Delay is always bad
policy :—

> " The work-deferrer never
> Sees full his barn, nor he that leaves work ever,
> And still is gadding out. Care-flying ease
> Gives labour ever competent increase :
> He that with doubts his needful business crosses
> Is always wrestling with uncertain losses."
> —C. 48-53.

Accordingly, on the principle of having all proper
implements of one's own, the poet proceeds to give
instructions for the most approved make of a wain, a
plough, a mortar, a pestle, and so forth. The time to
fell timber, so that it be not worm-eaten, and so that
it may not be cut when the sap is running, is when in
autumn the Dog-star, Sirius, " gets more night and less
day ;"—in other words, when the summer heats abate,
and men's bodies take a turn to greater lissomness and
moisture. The pestle and mortar prescribed were a
stone handmill or quern, for crushing and bruising corn
and other grain, and bring us back to days of very
primitive simplicity, though still in use in the days of
Aristophanes. So minute is the poet in his directions
for making the axle-tree of a waggon, that he recommends its length to be seven feet, but adds that it is
well to cut an eight-foot length, that one foot sawn off
may serve for the head of a mallet for driving in stakes.
The axles of modern carts are about six feet long.
But his great concern is, to give full particulars about

the proper wood and shape for the various parts of his
plough. The plough-tail (Virgil's "buris," Georg. i. 170)
is to be of ilex wood, which a servant of Athena — *i.e.*,
a carpenter — is to fasten with nails to the share-beam,
and fit to the pole. It is well, he says, to have two
ploughs, in case of an accident to a single one. And
whilst one of these was to have plough-tail, share-
beam, and pole all of one piece of timber, the other
was to be of three parts, each of different timber, and
all fastened with nails. This latter is apparently the
better of the two, that which is all of one wood being
a most primitive implement, simply "a forked bough."
The soundest poles are made of bay or elm, share-beams
of oak, and plough-tails of ilex oak. For draught
and yoking together, nine-year-old oxen are best, because, being past the mischievous and frolicsome age,
they are not likely to break the pole and leave the
ploughing in the middle. Directions follow this somewhat dry detail as to the choice of a ploughman :—

"In forty's prime thy ploughman ; one with bread
Of four-squared loaf in double portions fed.
He steadily will cut the furrow true,
Nor toward his fellows glance a rambling view,
Still on his task intent : a stripling throws
Heedless the seed, and in one furrow strows
The lavish handful twice, while wistful stray
His longing thoughts to comrades far away."
—E. 602-609.

The loaf referred to was scored crosswise, like the
Latin "quadra" or our cross-bun, and the object in
this case was easy and equal division of the slaves'

rations. Theocritus, xxiv. 136, speaks of "a big
Doric loaf in a basket, such as would safely satisfy a
garden-digger;" and it is probable that, in prescribing
a loaf with eight quarterings, Hesiod means "double
rations," thereby implying that it is good economy to
feed your men well, if you would have them work
well.

The poet next proceeds to advise that the cattle
should be kept in good condition, and ready for work,
when the migratory crane's cry bespeaks winter's
advent and the prospect of wet weather. Everything
should be in readiness for this; and it will not do to
rely on borrowing a yoke of oxen from a neighbour at
the busy time. The wideawake neighbour may up
and say,—

"Work up thyself a waggon of thine own,
For to the foolish borrower is not known
That each wain asks a hundred joints of wood:
These things ask forecast, and thou shouldst make good
At home, before thy need so instant stood."
—C. 122-126.

A farmer who knows what he is about will have,
Hesiod says, all his gear ready. He and his slaves
will turn to and plough, wet and dry, early and late,
working manfully themselves, and not forgetting to
pray Zeus and Demeter to bless the labour of their
hand, and bestow their fruits. An odd addition to the
farmer's staff is the slave who goes behind the plough
to break the clods, and *give trouble to the birds* by
covering up the seed. In Wilkinson's 'Ancient
Egyptians' (ii. 13), an engraving representing the

processes of ploughing and hoeing gives a slave in the rear with a wooden hoe, engaged in breaking the clods. A little further on, a reference to the same interesting work explains Hesiod's meaning where he says, that if ploughing is done at the point of midwinter, men will have to sit or stoop to reap (on account, it should seem, of the lowness of the ears), "enclosing but little round the hand, and often covered with dust while binding it up." To judge by the Egyptian paintings, wheat was reaped by men in an upright posture, because they cut the straw much nearer the ear than the ground. Of course, if the straw was very short, the reaper had to stoop, or to sit, if he liked it better. He is represented by Hesiod as seizing a handful of corn in his left hand, while he cuts it with his right, and binding the stalks in bundles in opposite directions, the handfuls being disposed alternately, stalks one way and ears the other. The basket of which Hesiod speaks as carrying the ears clipped from the straw, has its illustration also in the same pages. This is the explanation given also by Mr Paley in his notes. On the whole, the poet is strongly against late sowing, though he admits that if you can sow late in the dry, rainy weather in early spring may bring on the corn so as to be as forward as that which was early sown ;—

"So shall an equal crop thy time repair,
　With his who earlier launched the shining share."
　　　　　　　　　　　　　　　—E. 676, 677.

In this part of the 'Works' our poet is exceptionally matter-of-fact; but as he proceeds to tell what is

to be done and what avoided in the wintry season, he
becomes more amusing. He warns against the error
of supposing that this is the time for gossip at the
smithy, there being plenty of work for an active man
to do in the coldest weather. In fact, then is the
time for household work, and for so employing your
leisure

"That, famine-smitten, thou may'st ne'er be seen
To grasp a tumid foot with hand from hunger lean;"—
—E. 690, 691.

a figurative expression for a state of starvation, which
emaciates the hand and swells the foot by reason of
weakness. As a proper pendant to this sound advice,
Hesiod adds his much-admired description of winter,
the storms and cold of which he could thoroughly
speak of from the experience of a mountain residence
in Bœotia. This episode is so poetic,—even if over-
wrought in some portions,—that critics have suggested
its being a later addition of a rhapsodist of the post-
Hesiodic school; and there are two or three tokens
(e. g., the mention of "Lenaeon" as the month that
answers to our Christmastide and beginning of January, whereas the Bœotians knew no such name, but
called the period in question "Bucatius") which bespeak a later authorship. And yet a sensitiveness to
cold, and a lively description of its phenomena, is
quite in keeping with the poet's disparagement of
Ascra; and farther, it is quite possible that, *à propos*
of Hesiod and his works, theories of interpolation have
been suffered to overstep due limits. Inclination, and

absence of any certain data, combine to facilitate our
acceptance of this fine passage as the poet's own handi-
work. Indeed, it were a hard fate for any poet if, in
the lapse of years, his beauties were to be pronounced
spurious by hypercriticism, and his level passages alone
left to give an idea of his calibre. We give the description of winter from Elton's version:—

" Beware the January month ; beware
Those hurtful days, that keenly-piercing air
Which flays the steers, while frosts their horrors cast,
Congeal the ground, and sharpen every blast.
From Thracia's courser-teeming region sweeps
The northern wind, and, breathing on the deeps,
Heaves wide the troubled surge: earth, echoing, roars
From the deep forests and the sea-beat shores.
He from the mountain-top, with shattering stroke,
Rends the lofty pine, and many a branching oak
Hurls 'thwart the glen ; when sudden, from on high,
With headlong fury rushing down the sky,
The whirlwind stoops to earth ; then deepening round
Swells the loud storm, and all the boundless woods resound.
The beasts their cowering tails with trembling fold,
And shrink and shudder at the gusty cold.
Though thick the hairy coat, the shaggy skin,
Yet that all chilling breath shall pierce within.
Not his rough hide the ox can then avail,
The long-haired goat defenceless feels the gale ;
Yet vain the north wind's rushing strength to wound
The flock, with sheltering fleeces fenced around.
. . . .
And now the hornèd and unhornèd kind,
Whose lair is in the wood, sore famished grind
Their sounding jaws, and frozen and quaking fly,
Where oaks the mountain-dells imbranch on high ;

They seek to couch in thickets of the glen,
Or lurk deep sheltered in the rocky den.
*Like aged men who, propped on crutches, tread
Tottering, with broken strength and stooping head,*
So move the beasts of earth, and, creeping low,
Shun the white flakes and dread the drifting snow."
—E. 700-745.

The lines italicised scarcely realise the poet's comparison of the crouching beasts to three-footed old men, or old men crawling with the help of a stick, which in the original recalls, as Hesiod doubtless meant it to do, the famous local legend of the Sphinx.

"Now," adds the poet, "is the time to go warm-clad, thick-shod, and with a waterproof cape over the shoulders, and a fur cap, lined with felt, about the head and ears." He certainly knew how to take care of himself. But he is equally thoughtful for his hinds. When at this season the rain betokened by a misty morning sets in at night, and cold and wet interfere with husbandry, a time "severe to flocks, nor less to man severe," then, because workmen need more food in cold weather, but cattle, having little work by day and plenty of rest at night, can do with less,—

" Feed thy keen husbandmen with larger bread,
With half their provender thy steers be fed.
Them rest assists ; the night's protracted length
Recruits their vigour and supplies their strength.
This rule observe, while still the various earth
Gives every fruit and kindly seedling birth ;
Still to the toil proportionate the cheer,
The day to night, and equalise the year."
—E. 775-782.

And now the poet turns to vine-dressing. He dates the early spring by the rising of Arcturus, sixty days after the winter solstice (February 19), which is soon followed by the advent of the swallow. This is the season for vine-trimming; but when the snail (which Hesiod characteristically, and in language resembling that used in oracular responses, designates as "house-carrier") quits the earth and climbs the trees, to shelter itself from the Pleiads, then vine-culture must give place (about the middle of May) to the early harvest. Then must men rise betimes:—

"Lo! the third portion of thy labour's cares
 The early morn anticipating shares:
 In early morn the labour swiftly wastes,
 In early morn the speeded journey hastes,
 The time when many a traveller tracks the plain,
 And the yoked oxen bend them to the wain."
—E. 801-806.

A brief and picturesque episode follows about the permissible rest and enjoyment of the summer season, when artichokes flower, and the "cicala" (as Hesiod accurately puts it) pours forth "song from its wings" —the result of friction or vibration. "Then," he says, "fat kids, mellow wine, and gay maidens are fair relaxation for the sun-scorched rustic," who, however, is supposed to make merry with *temperate* cups, and to enjoy the cool shade and trickling rill quite as much as the grape-juice. Hesiod prescribes three cups of water to one of wine; and, as Cratinus's question in Athenæus — "Will it bear three parts water?"—suggests, only generous wine will stand such dilution. If such potations are ever seasonable, however, it will be in the greatest heat of summer, when the Dog Star burns. The rising of Orion is the time for threshing and winnowing (*i.e.*, about the middle of July); and this operation appears to have been performed by drawing over the corn the heavy-toothed plank or "tribulum," or trampling it by means of cattle on a smooth level threshing-floor. In some parts of Europe, Mr Paley informs us, the old process is still retained. After the corn has been winnowed, Hesiod counsels a revision of the household staff, in language of which Chapman catches the humour:—

"Make then thy man-swain one that hath no house,
Thy handmaid one that hath nor child nor spouse:
Handmaids that children have are ravenous.
A mastiff likewise nourish still at home,
Whose teeth are sharp and close as any comb,
And meat him well, to keep with stronger guard
The *day-sleep-night-wake man* from forth thy yard."
—C. 346-352.

When Sirius and Orion are in mid-heaven, and Arcturus is rising, then the grapes are to be gathered, so that Hesiod's vintage would be in the middle of September; and he prescribes exactly the process of (1) drying the grapes in the sun, (2) drying them in the shade to prevent fermentation, and (3) treading and squeezing out the wine:—

"The rosy-fingered morn the vintage calls;
Then bear the gathered grapes within thy walls.

> "Ten days and nights exposed the clusters lay,
> Basked in the radiance of each mellowing day.
> Let five their circling round successive run,
> Whilst lie thy grapes o'ershaded from the sun;
> The sixth express the harvest of the vine,
> And teach thy vats to foam with joy-inspiring wine."
> —E. 851-858.

When the Pleiads, Hyads, and Orion set, it is time to plough again. But not to go on a voyage! Though, as we have before stated, and as Hesiod seems particularly anxious to have it known, he was no sailor, our poet gives now directions how to keep boats and tackle safe and sound in the wintry season, by means of a rude breakwater of stones, and by taking the plug out of the keel to prevent its rotting. The best season for voyaging is between midsummer and autumn, he says; only it requires haste, to avoid the winter rains. The other and less desirable time is in spring, when the leaves at the end of a spray have grown to the length of a crow's foot — a comparative measurement, which Mr Paley observes is still retained in the popular name of some species of the ranunculus—crowfoot; but Hesiod calls this a "snatched voyage," and holds the love of gain that essays it foolhardy. He concludes his remarks on this head by prudent advice not to risk all your exports in one venture, all your eggs—as our homely proverb runs—in one basket:—

> "Trust not thy whole precarious wealth to sea,
> Tossed in the hollow keel: a portion send:
> Thy larger substance let the shore defend.

Fearful the losses of the ocean fall,
When on a fragile plank embarked thy all:
So bends beneath its weight the o'erburdened wain,
And the crushed axle spoils the scattered grain.
The golden mean of conduct should confine
Our every aim,—be moderation thine!"
—E. 954-962.

After this fashion the poet proceeds to give the advice on marriage which has been already quoted, and which probably belongs to an earlier portion of the poem. From this he turns to the duties of friendship, still regulated by caution and an eye to expediency. It is better to be reconciled to an old friend with whom you have fallen out than to contract new friendships; and, above all, to put a control on your countenance, that it may betray no reservations or misgivings. A careful and temperate tongue is commended, and geniality at a feast, especially a club feast, for

"When many guests combine in common fare,
Be not morose, nor grudge a liberal share:
Where all contributing the feast unite,
Great is the pleasure, and the cost is light."
—E. 1009-1012.

And now come some precepts of a ceremonial nature, touching what Professor Conington justly calls "smaller moralities and decencies," some of which, it has been suggested, savour of Pythagorean or of Judaic obligation, whilst all bespeak excessive superstition. Prayers with unwashen hands, fording a river without propitiatory prayer, paring the nails off your "*bunch of fives*" (*i.e.*, your five fingers*) at a feast after sacrifice, lifting the can above the bowl at a banquet,—all these acts of commission and omission provoke, says Hesiod, the wrath of the gods. Some of his precepts have a substratum of common sense, but generally they can only be explained by his not desiring to contravene the authority of custom; and, in fact, he finishes his second part with a reason for the observance of such rules and cautions:—

" Thus do, and shun the ill report of men.
Light to take up, it brings the bearer pain,
And is not lightly shaken off; nor dies
The rumour that from many lips doth rise,
But, like a god, all end of time defies."—D.

And now comes the closing portion of the poem, designated by Chapman "Hesiod's Book of Days," and, in point of fact, a calendar of the lucky and unlucky days of the lunar month, apparently as connected with the various worships celebrated on those days. The poet divides the month of thirty days, as was the use at Athens much later, into three decades. The thirtieth of the month is the best day for overlooking farm-work done, and allotting the rations for the month coming on; and it is a holiday, too, in the law-courts. The seventh of the month is specially lucky as Apollo's birthday; the sixth unlucky for birth or marriage of girls, probably because the birthday of the virgin Artemis, his sister. The fifth is very unlucky, because on it Horcus, the genius who punishes per-

---

* " A slang term for the fists, in use among pugilists."—See Paley's note on v. 712.

jury, and not, as Virgil supposed, the Roman Orcus or
Hades, was born, and taken care of by the Erinnyes.
The seventeenth was lucky for bringing in the corn to
the threshing-floor, and for other works, because it was
the festival-day, in one of the months, of Demeter
and Cora, or Proserpine. The fourth was lucky for
marriages, perhaps because sacred to Aphrodite and
Hermes. Hesiod lays down the law, however, of
these days without giving much enlightenment as to
the "why" or "wherefore," and our knowledge from
other sources does not suffice to explain them all. A
fair specimen of this calendar is that which we proceed
to quote :—

> "The eighth, nor less the ninth, with favouring skies
> Speeds of th' increasing month each rustic enterprise :
> And on the eleventh let thy flocks be shorn,
> And on the twelfth be reaped thy laughing corn :
> Both days are good ; yet is the twelfth confessed
> More fortunate, with fairer omen blest.
> On this the air-suspended spider treads,
> In the full noon, his fine and self-spun threads ;
> And the wise emmet, tracking dark the plain,
> Heaps provident the store of gathered grain.
> On this let careful woman's nimble hand
> Throw first the shuttle and the web expand."
> —E. 1071-1082.

Hesiod's account of the twenty-ninth of the month
is also a characteristic passage, not without a touch of
the oracular and mysterious. "The prudent secret,"
he says, "is to few confessed." "One man praises one
day, another another, but few know them." "Some-

times a day is a stepmother, sometimes a mother." "Blest and fortunate he who knowingly doeth all with an eye to these days, unblamed by the immortals, discerning omens and avoiding transgression."

Such is the appropriate ending of Hesiod's didactic poem—a termination which ascribes prosperity in agricultural pursuits to ascertainment of the will of the gods, and avoidance of even unwitting transgression of their festivals. The study of omens, the poet would have it understood, is the way to be safe in these matters.

The 'Works and Days' possesses a curious interest as Hesiod's most undoubted production, and as the earliest sample of so-called didactic poetry; nor is it fair or just to speak of this poem as an ill-constructed, loose-hanging concatenation of thoughts and hints on farming matters, according as they come uppermost. That later and more finished didactic poems have only partially and exceptionally borrowed Hesiod's manner or matter does not really detract from the interest of a poem which, as far as we know, is the first in classical literature to afford internal evidence of the writer's mind and thoughts,—the first to teach that *subjectivity*, in which to many readers lies the charm and attraction of poetry. No doubt Hesiod's style and manner betoken a very early and rudimentary school; but few can be insensible to the quaintness of his images, the "Dutch fidelity" (to borrow a phrase of Professor Conington) of his minute descriptions, or, lastly, the point and terseness of his maxims. To these the foregoing chapter on the 'Works and Days' has been unable to do justice, because it seemed of more consequence to show the connection and sequence of the parts and episodes of that work. It is proposed, therefore, in the brief chapter next following, to examine "the Proverbial Philosophy of Hesiod," which is chiefly, if not entirely, found in the poem we have been discussing.

CHAPTER III.

HESIOD'S PROVERBIAL PHILOSOPHY.

A CHIEF token of the antiquity of Hesiod's 'Works and Days' is his use of familiar proverbs to illustrate his vein of thought, and to attract a primitive audience. The scope and structure of his other extant poems are not such as to admit this mode of illustration; but the fact, that amidst the fragments which remain of his lost poems are preserved several maxims and saws of practical and homely wisdom, shows that this use of proverbs was characteristic of his poetry, or that his imitators—if we suppose these lost poems not to have been really his—at all events held it to be so. It is, perhaps, needless to remark that the poems of Homer are full of like adagial sentences—so much so, indeed, that James Duport, the Greek professor at Cambridge, published in 1680 an elaborate parallelism of the proverbial philosophy of the Iliad and Odyssey, with the adages as well of sacred as of profane writers. Other scholars have since followed his lead, and elucidated the same common point in the father of Greek poetry, and those who have opened a like vein in other nations and languages. Obviously an appeal to this terse and easily-remembered and retained wisdom of the ancients is adapted to the needs of an early stage of literature; and its kinship, apparent or real, to the brief "dicta" of the oracles of antiquity, would constitute a part of its weight and popularity with an audience of wonder-stricken listeners. And so we come to see the fitness of such bards as Homer and Hesiod garnishing their poems with these gems of antique proverbial wisdom, each drawing from a store that was probably hereditary, and pointing a moral or establishing a truth by neat and timely introduction of saws that possessed a weight not unlike that of texts of Scripture to enforce a preacher's drift. It is, furthermore, a minor argument for the common date of these famous poets, that both Homer and Hesiod constantly recur to the use of adages. With the latter the vein is not a little curious. The honest thrift-loving poet of Ascra has evidently stored up maxims, on the one hand of homely morality and good sense, and on the other of shrewdness and self-interest. He draws upon a rare stock of proverbial authority for justice, honour, and good faith, but he also falls back upon a well-chosen supply of brief and telling saws to affirm the policy of "taking care of number one," and is provided with short rules of action and conduct, which do credit to his observation and study of the ways of the world. If, as we have seen in his autobiography (if we may so call the 'Works and Days'), his life was a series of chronic wrestlings with a worthless brother and unjust judges, it is all the more natural that his stock of proverbs should partake of the twofold character indicated; and we proceed to illustrate both sides of it in their order.

In distinguishing the two kinds of contention, Hesiod ushers in a familiar proverb by words which have themselves taken adagial rank. "This contention," he says, "is good for mortals" ('Works and Days,' 24-26)—viz., "when potter vies with potter, craftsman with craftsman, beggar is emulous of beggar, and bard of bard." Pliny the younger, in a letter on the death of Silius Italicus, uses the introductory words of Hesiod à propos of the rivalry of friends, in provoking each other to the quest of a name and fame that may survive their perishable bodies;[*] and Aristotle and Plato quote word for word the lines respecting "two of a trade" to which it will be observed that Hesiod attaches a nobler meaning than that which has become associated with them in later days. He seems to appeal to the people's voice, succinctly gathered up into a familiar saw, for the confirmation of his argument, that honest emulation is both wholesome and profitable. The second of Hesiod's adages has an even higher moral tone, and conveys the lesson of temperance in its broadest sense, by declaring

"That *half* is more than *all;* true gain doth dwell
  In feasts of herbs, mallow, and asphodel."—D.

Here the seeming paradox of the first portion of the couplet is justified and explained by Cicero's remark that men know not "how great a revenue consists in

[*] Epist. III., vii. 15.

moderation;" and whilst in the first clause a sound mind is the end proposed, the latter part evidently has reference to the frugal diet, which bespeaks contentment and an absence of covetousness, such as breathes in Horace's prayer:—

> "Let olives, endives, mallows light
> Be all my fare,"—
> —Odes, I. 31, 15 (Theod. Martin).

and which, moreover, favours health and a sound body. It is unnecessary to point out the similarity of this proverb to that of Solomon respecting the "dinner of herbs," or to our own adage that "enough is as good as a feast;" but it may be pertinent to note that this Hesiodian maxim is, like the former, quoted by Plato, who in his Laws (iii. 690) explains Hesiod's meaning, "that when the whole was injurious and the half moderate, then the moderate was more and better than the immoderate." The next which presents itself in the 'Works and Days' owes its interest as much to the fact that it occurs almost *totidem verbis* in Homer, as to its resemblance to a whole host of later proverbs and adages amongst all nations. When Hesiod would fain enforce the advantage of doing right, and acting justly, without constraint, he, as it were, glances at the case of those who do not see this till justice has taught them its lesson, and says, in the language of proverb,

> "The fool first suffers, and is after wise."
> —'Works and Days,' 218.

In the 17th Book of the Iliad, Homer has the same

expression, save in the substitution of the word "acts" for "suffers;" and it is exceedingly probable that both adapted to their immediate purposes the words of a pre-existing proverb.* Hesiod had already glanced at the same proverb, when, in v. 89 of the 'Works and Days,' he said of the improvident Epimetheus that "he first took the gift "(Pandora)," and after grieved;" and it is probable that we have in it the germ of very many adagial expressions about the teaching of experience—such as those about "the stung fisherman," "the burnt child," and "the scalded cat" of the Latin, English, and Spanish languages respectively. The Ojis, according to Burton, say, "He whom a serpent has bitten, dreads a slow-worm." Of a kindred tone of high heathen morality are several proverbial expressions in the 'Works and Days' touching uprightness and justice in communities and individuals. Thus in one place we read that

"Oft the crimes of one destructive fall,
The crimes of one are visited on all."
—E. 319, 320.

In another, that mischief and malice recoil on their author:—

"Whoever forgeth for another ill,
With it himself is overtaken still;
In ill men run on that they most abhor;
Ill counsel worst is to the counsellor."
—Chapman.

* Livy has "Eventus stultorum magister;" and the Proverbs of Solomon, xx. 2, 3—"A prudent man foreseeth the evil and hideth himself; but the simple pass on and are punished."

And in a third, that
"Far best
Is heaven-sent wealth without reproach possest."

The second of these sentences recalls the story of the "Bull of Phalaris;" whilst another, not yet noticed, according to Elton's version, runs on this wise:—

"Who fears his oath shall leave a name to shine
With brightening lustre through his latest line."
—E. 383, 384.

More literally rendered, the sentence might read, "Of a man that regardeth his oath the seed is more blessed in the aftertime;" and so rendered, it curiously recalls the answer of the oracle to Glaucus in Herodotus (vi. 86), where the Greek words are identical with Hesiod's, and either denote an acquaintance, in the Pythoness, with the 'Works and Days,' or a common source whence both she and Hesiod drew. We give Juvenal's account of the story of Glaucus, from Hodgson's version:—

"The Pythian priestess to a Spartan sung,
While indignation raised her awful tongue:
'The time will come when e'en thy thoughts unjust,
Thy hesitation to restore the trust,
Thy purposed fraud shall make atonement due—
Apollo speaks it, and his voice is true.'
Scared at this warning, he who sought to try
If haply Heaven might wink at perjury,
Alive to fear, though still to virtue dead,
Gave back the treasure to preserve his head.
Vain hope, by reparation now too late,
To loose the bands of adamantine fate!

> By swift destruction seized, the caitiff dies,
> Swept from the earth: nor he sole sacrifice—
> One general doom o'erwhelms his cursed line,
> And verifies the judgment of the shrine."
>
> —P. 251, 252.

Within a couple of lines of the proverb last cited occurs a maxim almost scriptural in its phraseology. "Wickedness," sings the poet, "you might choose in a heap; level is the path, and it lies hard at hand." One is reminded of the "broad and narrow roads" in our Saviour's teaching; and the lines which follow, and enforce the earnest struggle which alone can achieve the steep ascent, have found an echo in many noble outbursts of after-poetry. The passage in Tennyson's Ode, which expands the sentiment, is sufficiently well known, but perhaps it is itself suggested by the 20th fragment of Simonides, which may be freely translated:—

> "List an old and truthful tale,—
>   Virtue dwells on summits high,
> Sheer and hard for man to scale,
>   Where the goddess doth not fail
>   Her pure precincts, ever nigh,
>
> Unrevealed to mortal sight,
>   Unrevealed, save then alone
> When some hero scales her height,
> Whom heart-vexing toil for right
>   Bringeth up to virtue's throne." *

---

* Tennyson's Ode on the Death of the Duke of Wellington:—
  " He that ever follows her commands,
  Or with toil of heart and knees and hands,

Of a less exalted tone is the famous graduation of man's wisdom, which declares "that man far best who can conceive and carry out with foresight a wise counsel; next in order, him who has the sense to value and heed such counsel; whilst he who can neither initiate it, nor avail himself of it when thrown in his way, is to all intents worthless and good for nothing."— ('Works and Days,' 294-297.) This passage, however, has been thought worthy of citation by Aristotle. Another passage of proverbial character, but subordinate moral tone, is that which declares—

" Lo ! the best treasure is a frugal tongue ;
The lips of moderate speech with grace are hung."
— -E. 1005, 1006.

And a little further on an adage of mixed character, moral and utilitarian, deifies the offspring of our unruly member, by saying—

" No rumour wholly dies, once bruited wide,
But deathless like a goddess doth abide."—D.

When we turn to the other class of adages—those which syllable the teaching of common-sense—we are struck more by the poet's shrewdness than his morality. The end of all his precepts is, " Brother, get rich ;" or "Brother, avoid poverty and famine." Even the worship and offerings of the gods are inculcated with an

---

Through the long gorge to the far light hath won
His path upward, and prevailed.
Shall find the toppling crags of duty sealed
Are close beside the shining table-lands
To which our God Himself is moon and sun."

eye to being able "to buy up the land of others, and
not others thine." (341). He says, indeed, in v. 686,
that "money is life to miserable men," in much the
same terms as Pindar after him; but this is only as a
dissuasive from unseasonable voyages, and because "in
all things the fitting season is best." In effect he
upholds the maxim that "money makes the man,"
though it is but fair to add that he prescribes right
means to that end. To get rich, a man must work:—

"Famine evermore
Is natural consort to the idle boor."—C.

"Hard work will best uncertain fortune mend."—D.

He must save, too, on the principle that "many a little
makes a mickle," or, as Hesiod hath it,

"Little to little added, if oft done,
In small time makes a good possession."—C.

It is no use, he sagaciously adds, to *spare the liquor
when the cask is empty:—*

"When broached, or at the lees, no care be thine
To save the cask, but spare the middle wine;"
—E. 503, 504.

nor to procrastinate, because

"Ever with loss the putter-off contends,"
—413.

and the man that would thrive must take time by the
forelock, repeating to himself, as well as to his slaves
at midsummer,—

"The summer day
Endures not ever: toil ye while ye may,"
—E. 698, 699.

and rising betimes in the morning, on the faith that

"The morn the third part of thy work doth gain;
The morn makes short thy way, makes short thy pain."—C.

Shrewd and practical as all this teaching is, its author deprecates anything that is not honest and straightforward. "Dishonest gains," he declares in v. 352, "are tantamount to losses;" and perhaps his experience of the detriment of such ill gains to his brother enabled him to judge of their hurtfulness the more accurately. Referable to this experience is a maxim that is certainly uncomplimentary to brotherly love and confidence:—

"As if in joke, that he no slight may feel,
Call witnesses, if you with brother deal."
—D. 371.

And there is a latent distrust of kinsfolk and connections involved in another proverb:—

"When on your home falls unforeseen distress,
Half-clothed come neighbours: kinsmen stay to dress."
—D. 345.

Perhaps his bardic character won him the goodwill of his neighbours, and so he estimated them as he found them; for he says a little further on, with considerable fervour—

"He hath a treasure, by his fortune signed,
That hath a neighbour of an honest mind."
—C. 347.

And in his treatment of these neighbours there was, to judge by his teaching, a very fair amount of liberality, though scarcely that high principle of benevolence which is content "to give, hoping nothing again." Self-interest, indeed, as might be expected, leavens the mass of his precepts of conduct, which may be characterised as a good workaday code for the citizen of a little narrow world, shut up within Beotian mountains. We laugh at the suspicion that animates some, and the homeliness of others, but cannot fail withal to be captivated perforce by the ingenuousness with which the poet speaks his inner mind, and pretends to no higher philosophy than one of self-defence. In the line which follows the couplet last quoted, and which says that "where neighbours are what they should be, not an ox would be lost," for the whole village would turn out to catch the thief,—it has been surmised that there is allusion to an early "association for the prosecution of felons" in the Æolian colony from which Hesiod's father had come; but these glosses of commentators and scholiasts only spoil the simplicity of the poet's matter-of-fact philosophy, which in the instance referred to did but record what Themistocles afterwards seems to have seen, when, as a recommendation to a field for sale, he advertised that it had "a good neighbour."

Though the 'Theogony' is, from its nature and scope, by no means a storehouse of proverbs like the 'Works and Days,' it here and there has allusions and references to an already existing stock of such maxims. Where, in pointing a moral *à propos* of Pandora, he takes up his parable against women, and likens them to the drones,

"Which gather in their greedy maw the spoils
Of others' labour,"—
—E. 797, 798.

Hesiod has in his mind's eye that ancient proverb touching "one sowing and another reaping," which Callimachus gives as follows in his hymn to Ceres (137)—

"And those who ploughed the field shall reap the corn"—

but which, in some shape or other, must have existed previously even to Hesiod's date. In most modern languages it has its counterpart; and it was recognised and applied by our Lord, and His apostle St Paul.* Earlier in the poem, the saw that "Blest is he whom the Muses love" is probably pre-Hesiodian; but it is too obviously a commonplace of poets in general to deserve commemoration as a proverb. We cannot cite any adages from 'The Shield,' and an examination of 'The Fragments' adds but few to the total of Hesiod's stock. These few are chiefly from the 'Maxims of Chiron,' supposed to have been dictated by that philosophic Centaur to his pupil Achilles. One of these, preserved by Harpocration from an oration of Hyperides, may be thus translated:—

"Works for the young, counsels for middle age;
The old may best in vows and prayers engage."

Another savours of the philosophy of the 'Works and Days:'—

* St Matt. xxv. 24; Gal. vi. 7; 2 Cor. ix. 6.

"Gifts can move gods, and gifts our godlike kings."

Whilst a third might well be a stray line from one of the exhortations to Perses: for it deprecates the preference of a shadow to a substance in some such language as this:—

"Only a fool will fruits in hand forego,
That he the charm of doubtful chase may know."

Another proverb, preserved by Cicero in a letter to Atticus,[*] looks very like Hesiod's, though the orator and critical man of letters dubs it "pseudo-Hesiodian." It bids us "not decide a case until both sides have been heard." And yet another saw, referred to the Ascræan sage, appears to us in excellent keeping with the maxims respecting industry and hard work which abound in his great didactic poem. We are indebted for it to Xenophon's Memorabilia, and it may be Englished—

"Seek not the smooth, lest thou the rough shouldst find,"—

an exhortation in accord with the fine passage in the 'Works and Days,' which represents Virtue and Excellence seated aloft on heights difficult to climb.

Perhaps also the following extracts from the extant fragments of the 'Catalogue of Women,' though not succinct enough to rank as adages, may lay some claim to containing jets and sparkles of adagial wisdom. The first, taken from the pages of Athenaeus,[†] concerns wine that maketh sorry, as well as glad, the heart of man:—

[* vii 18, 1.]   [† x. 428.]

"What joy, what pain doth Dionysus give
To men who drink to excess. For wine to such
Acts insolently, binds them hand and foot,
Yea, tongue and mind withal, in bondage dire,
Ineffable! Sleep only stands their friend."—D.

The second is a curious relic of the ancient notions about comparative longevity:—

"Nine generations lives the babbling crow
Of old men's life; the lively stag outlasts
Four crow-lives, and the raven thrice the stag's.
Nine raven's terms the phœnix numbers out;
And we, the long-tressed nymphs, whose sire is Zeus,
By ten times more the phœnix life exceed."—D.

Enough, however, has been set down of Hesiod's proverbial philosophy, to show that herein consists one of his titles to a principal place among didactic poets. A plain blunt man, and a poet of the people, he knew how and when to appeal with cogency to that "wisdom of many and wit of one," which has been styled by our own proverb-collector, **James Howell**, "the people's voice."

CHAPTER IV.

THE THEOGONY.

THE geographer Pausanias was the first to cast a doubt upon the received belief of the ancients that the 'Theogony' and the 'Works and Days' originated from one and the same author. On the other hand, Herodotus attributed to Hesiod the praise of having been one of the earliest systematisers of a national mythology; and Plato in his Dialogues has references to the 'Theogony' of Hesiod, which apparently correspond with passages in the work that has come down to us as such. Unless, therefore, there is strong internal evidence of separate authorship in the two poems, the testimony of a writer four hundred years before Christ is entitled to outweigh that of one living two hundred years after. But so far from such internal evidence being forthcoming, it would be easy to enumerate several strong notes of resemblance, which would go far towards establishing a presumption that both were from the same hand. The same economical spirit which actuates the poet of the 'Works' is visible also in the 'Theogony,' where the head and front of Pandora's offending is, that the "beauteous evil," woman, is a drone in the hive, and consumes the fruits of man's labour without adding to them. The author of the 'Theogony' holds in exceptionally high esteem the wealth-giving divinity Plutus, and this is quite consistent with the hereditary and personal antipathy to poverty and its visitations so manifest in the bard of the 'Works.' Again, there is reason to believe that the proper commencement of the 'Works and Days' —which, to translate the Greek idiom, might run, "Well, it seems that after all Contention is of two kinds, and not of one only" (v. 11)—is nothing less than the poet's correction of a statement he had made in his poem on the generation of the gods, that Eris, or Contention, was one and indivisible, the daughter of Night, and the mother of an uncanny progeny, beginning with Trouble and ending with Oath.* We might add, too, curious coincidences of expression and verse-structure, such as the use of a characteristic epithet standing by itself for the substantive which it would commonly qualify (e. g., "the boneless" to represent "the caterpillar," and "the silvery" for "the sea"), and the peculiarity of the commencement of three consecutive lines with one and the same word. Instances of both are common to the two poems. But for the purposes of the present volume it is perhaps sufficient to rest our acquiescence in a common authership upon the plausibility and reasonableness of Bishop Thirlwall's view, that Hesiod, living amidst a people rich in sacred and oracular poetry, and engaged for the

* See Theog., v. 225.

most part in husbandry, "collected for it in a fuller and a more graceful body the precepts with which the simple wisdom of their forefathers had ordered their rural labours and their domestic life;" at the same time that, "from the songs of their earlier bards, and the traditions of their temples, he drew the knowledge of nature and of superhuman things which he delivered in the popular form of the 'Theogony.'" *

Of the aim which he proposed to himself in that ancient poem, no better description has been given than Mr Grote's, who designates it as "an attempt to cast the divine functions into a systematic sequence." The work of Homer and Hesiod was, to reduce to system the most authentic traditions about the Hellenic gods and demi-gods, and to consolidate a catholic belief in the place of conflicting local superstitions. So far as we are able to judge, Homer's share in the task consisted in the passing notices of gods and goddesses which are scattered up and down the Iliad and the Odyssey. For Hesiod may be claimed the first incorporation and enumeration of the generation and genealogy of the gods and goddesses in a coherent system; and so it was from his 'Theogony,' as Mr Grote has shown, that "men took their information respecting their theogonic antiquities; that sceptical pagans, and later assailants of paganism, derived their subjects of attack; and that, to understand what Plato deprecated and Xenophanes denounced, the Hesiodic stories must be recounted in naked simplicity." † Whence he derived his information, which is older than the so-called

* 'Hist. of Greece, I., c. vi. † Ibid., L 15, 16.

Orphic Theogony—whether from Egypt, India, and
Persia, or, as some have thought, from the Mosaic
writings—it is lost labour to inquire. He certainly
systematised and consolidated the mass of traditions,
which came to his hand a more or less garbled and
distorted collection of primitive and nearly universal
legendary lore. An especial interest must therefore
attach to the study of his scheme and method, and it
must be enhanced by the position which antiquity
has almost unanimously accorded to him, in the history
of its earliest poetry and religion.

Hesiod's 'Theogony' consists of three divisions: a
cosmogony, or creation of the world, its powers, and
its fabric; a theogony proper, recording the history
of the dynasties of Cronus and Zeus; and a fragmentary generation of heroes, sprung from the intercourse
of mortals with immortals. Hesiod and his contemporaries considered that in their day Jupiter or Zeus
was the lord of Olympus; but it was necessary to
chronicle the antecedents of his dynasty, and hence the
account of the stages and revolutions which had led up
to the established order under which Hesiod's generation found itself. And so, after a preface containing
amongst other matters the episode of the Muses' visit
to the shepherd-poet, at which we glanced in Chapter
I., Hesiod proceeds to his proper task, and represents
Chaos as primeval, and Earth, Tartarus, and Eros
(Love), as coming next into existence:—

              "Love then arose,
Most beauteous of immortals; he at once
Of every god and every mortal man

Unnerves the limbs, dissolves the wiser breast
By reason steeled, and quells the very soul."
—E. 171-175.

At first Chaos spontaneously produces Erebus and Night, the latter of whom gives birth to Ether and Day; whilst Earth creates in turn the heaven, the mountains, and the sea, the cosmogony so far corresponding generally with the Mosaic. But at this point Eros or Love begins to work. The union of Earth with Heaven results in the birth of Oceanus and the Titans, the Cyclopes, and the hundred-handed giants. The sire of so numerous a progeny, and first ruler of creation, Uranus, conceiving that his sovereignty is imperilled by his offspring, resorts to the expedient of relodging each child, as soon as it is born, within the bowels of its mother, Earth. Groaning under such a burden, she arms her youngest and wiliest son, Cronus, with a sickle of her own product, iron, and hides him in an ambush with a view to his mutilating his sire. The conspiracy is justified on the principle of retributive justice. Uranus is disabled and dethroned, and, by a not very clear nor presentable legend, the foam-born goddess Aphrodite is fabled to have sprung from his mutilation. Here is the poet's account of her rise out of the sea:—

"So severing with keen steel
The sacred spoils, he from the continent
Amid the many surges of the sea
Hurled them. Full long they drifted o'er the deeps,
Till now swift-circling a white foam arose
From that immortal substance, and a nymph

Was nourished in their midst. The wafting waves
First bore her to Cythera the divine:
To wave-encircled Cyprus came she then,
And forth emerged a goddess in the charms
Of awful beauty. *Where her delicate feet
Had pressed the sands, green herbage flowering sprang.*
Her Aphrodite gods and mortals name,
The foam-born goddess: and her name is known
As Cytherea with the blooming wreath,
For that she touched Cythera's flowery coast;
And Cypris, for that on the Cyprian shore
She rose amid the multitude of waves.
Love tracked her steps, and beautiful Desire
Pursued; while soon as born she bent her way
Towards heaven's assembled gods: her honours these
From the beginning: whether gods or men
Her presence bless, to her the portion falls
Of virgin whisperings and alluring smiles,
And smooth deceits, and gentle ecstasy,
And dalliance and the blandishments of love."
—F. 258-283.

The concluding verses of this passage are notable as enumerating the fabled assessors of Venus; and the italicised lines, which find modern parallels in Milton, Scott, and Tennyson,* may have suggested the invo-

* " Now when as sacred light began to dawn
In Eden on the humid flowers that breathed
Their morning incense, when all things that breathe
From the earth's great altar send up silent praise
To the Creator;" &c.
—Paradise Lost, ix.

" A foot more light, a step more true,
Ne'er from the heath-flower dash'd the dew;
E'en the slight harebell raised its head
Elastic from her airy tread."
—Lady of the Lake, I. 18.

cation of the beniguant goddess in the opening of
Lucretius : —

"Before thee, goddess, thee ! the winds are hushed,
Before thy coming are the clouds dispersed ;
The plastic earth spreads flowers before thy feet ;
Thy presence makes the plains of ocean smile,
And sky shines placid with diffused light."
— Lucret. i. 7-12 (Johnson).

By the act of Cronus, the Titans, released from durance, arose to a share in the deliverer's dynasty, the Cyclopes and giants still, it would seem, remaining shut up in their prison-house. But before the poet proceeds to the history of this dynasty and succession of rulers, he apparently conceives it to be his duty to go through the generations of the elder deities with a genealogical

"But light as any wind that blows,
So fleetly did she stir ;
The flower she touched on dipt and rose,
And turned to look at her."
—Tennyson : 'The Talking Oak.'

Even more to the point, which is the charm to create verdure and flower-growth which pertains to Aphrodite's feet, are the following citations from Ben Jonson and Wordsworth :—

"Here she was wont to go, and here, and here,
Just where those daisies, pinks, and violets grow ;
The world may find the spring by following her,
For other print her aery steps ne'er left.
And where she went the flowers took thickest root,
As she had sowed them with her odorous foot."
—Jonson : 'Sad Shepherd,' l. 1.

"Flowers laugh before thee in their beds,
And fragrance in thy footing treads."
—Wordsworth : 'Ode to Duty.'

minuteness which, it must be confessed, is now and
then tedious; though, on the other hand, there are occasional points of interest in the process, which would
be interminable if not so relieved. It is curious, for
example, to find "the Hesperian maids"—

> "Whose charge o'ersees the fruits of bloomy gold
> Beyond the sounding ocean, the fair trees
> Of golden fruitage"—
>
> —E. 293-297.

ranked with Death, and Sleep, and Gloom and its
kindred, as the unbegotten brood of Night. Possibly
the clue is to be found in Hesiod's having a glimmer-
ing of the Fall and its consequences, because death and
woe were in the plucking of the fruit of "that forbid-
den tree." Again, from the union of Nereus, the sea-
god *par excellence*, and eldest offspring of Pontus, one
of the original powers, with the Oceanid, Doris, are
said to have sprung the fifty Nereids, whose names,
taken from some characteristic of the sea—its wonders,
its treasures, and its good auguries—correspond in
many instances with Homer's list in the Iliad (xviii.
39-48), and point to a pre-existent legend approached
by both poets. In due order, also, are recorded the
children of Tethys and the Titan Oceanus,—to wit,
the endless rivers and springs, and the water-nymphs,
or Oceanids, whose function is to preside over these,
and to convey nourishment from the Sire to all things
living. As to the list of rivers, it is noticeable that
Hesiod includes the Nile, known to Homer only by
the name of Ægyptus—and the Eridanus, supposed to

represent the Rhodanus or Rhone; also that the rivers
of Greece appear to be slighted in comparison with
those of Asia Minor and the Troad—a circumstance to
be accounted for by the Asiatic origin of the poet's
father, which would explain his completer geographical knowledge of the colonies than of the mother
country. The names of the water nymphs are referable to islands and continents—*e. g.*, Europa, Asia,
Doris, Persia—or to physical characteristics, such as
clearness, turbidness, violet hue, and the like. But
the poet gives a good reason for furnishing only a
selection:—

    " More remain untold. Three thousand nymphs
    Of Oceanic line, in beauty tread
    With ample step, and far and wide dispersed
    Haunt the green earth and azure depth of lakes,
    A blooming race of glorious goddesses
    As many rivers also yet untold,
    Rushing with hollow dashing sound, were born
    To awful Tethys, but their every name
    Is not for mortal man to memorate,
    Arduous, yet known to all the dwellers round."
                             —E. 492-501.

We must not trespass upon our readers' patience, by
enumerating with the conscientious genealogist the
progeny of the rest of the Titans. Two goddesses,
however, stand out from amidst one or other of these
broods, as of more special note, and more direct bearing
upon the world's government and order. Asteria, the
goddess of stars, a Titanid in the second generation,
bears to Perses, a god of light, and a Titan of the original
stock, one only daughter, Hecate. The attributes of

this goddess, as described by Hesiod, are so discrepant
from those ascribed to her by later poets, as to afford
strong proof of the antiquity of this poem. She is not,
as in later poetry, the patron of magic arts, but the
goddess who blesses labour and energy, in field, senate,
and forum :—

> "When the mailed men rise
> To deadly battle, comes the goddess prompt
> To whom she wills, bids rapid victory
> Await them, and extends the wreath of fame.
> She sits upon the sacred judgment-seat
> Of venerable monarchs. She is found
> Propitious when in solemn games the youth
> Contending strive ; there is the goddess nigh
> With succour ; he whose hardiment and strength
> Victorious prove, with ease the graceful palm
> Achieving, joyous o'er his father's age,
> Sheds a bright gleam of glory. She is known
> To them propitious, who the fiery steed
> Rein in the course, and them who labouring cleave
> Through the blue watery waste the untractable way."
> —E. 581-595.

The other goddess, Styx, a daughter of Oceanus, is
memorable not more for her own prominent position
in ancient fable, than for having amongst her offspring those iron-handed ministers of Jove, Strength
(Kratos) and Force (Bia), whom the classical reader
meets again in the opening of the 'Prometheus' of
Æschylus. Their nearness to Zeus is ascribed by
Hesiod to the decision with which their mother
espoused his cause in the struggle with Cronus and the
Titans :—

> "Lo! then incorruptible Styx the first,
> Swayed by the awful counsels of her sire,
> Stood on Olympus and her sons beside;
> There graced with honour and with goodly gifts,
> Her Zeus ordained the great tremendous oath
> Of deities; her sons for evermore
> Indwellers in the heavens. Alike to all,
> Even as he pledged his sacred word, the god
> Performed; so reigned he strong in might and power."
> —E. 537-545.

But here Hesiod has been anticipating the sequence of events, and forestalling, to this extent, the second stage of the poem. According to Hesiod, Cronus or Saturn was alive to the faults of his sire's policy of self-protection, and conceived an improvement in the means of checking revolutionary development on the part of his offspring, by imprisoning them in his own bowels rather than their mother's. Mindful of the destiny that "to his own child he should bow down his strength," he proceeded to swallow up his progeny with such regularity, that the maternal feelings of his consort, Rhea, roused her to a spirit of opposition. When about to be delivered of her sixth child, Zeus, she called in the aid of her parents, Heaven and Earth, in the concealment of his birth:—

> "And her they sent to Lyctus, to the clime
> Of fruitful Crete, and when her hour was come,
> The birth of Zeus, her youngest born, then Earth
> Took to herself the mighty babe, to rear
> With nurturing softness, in the spacious isle
> Of Crete: so came she then, transporting him
> Swift through the darksome air, to Lyctus first,

And thence upbearing in her arms, concealed
Beneath the sacred ground in sunless cave,
Where shagged with densest woods the Ægean mount
Impends. But to the imperial son of heaven,
Whilom the King of gods, a stone she gave
Inwrapt in infant swathes, and this with grasp
Eager he snatched, and in his ravening breast
Conveyed away; unhappy! nor once thought
That for the stone his child remained behind
Invincible, secure; who soon with hands
Of strength o'ercoming him, should cast him forth
From glory, and himself the immortals rule."
—E. 641-659.

As the gods in ancient mythology grow apace, Zeus is soon ripe for the task of aiding his mother, whose craft persuades Cronus to disgorge first the stone which he had mistaken for his youngest-born, and then the five children whom he had previously devoured. A stone, probably meteoric, was shown at Delphi in Pausanias's day as the stone in question, and an object of old memorial to the devout Greek. The rescued brethren at once take part with their deliverer. The first act of Zeus was, as we have seen, to advance Force and Strength, with their brothers Victory and Rivalry, to the dignity of "a body-guard," and to give their mother Styx the style and functions of "oath-sanctioner." His next was to free from the prison to which their father Uranus had consigned them, the hundred-handed giants, and the Cyclopes, who furnished his artillery of lightnings and hot thunderbolts. His success in the struggle was assured by the oracles of Gæa (Earth), if only he could

band these towers of strength and muscularity against
Cronus and his Titans; and so the battle was set in
array, and a fierce war ensued—

> "Each with each
> Ten years and more the furious battle joined
> Unintermitted; nor to either host
> Was issue of stern strife nor end; alike
> Did either stretch the limit of the war."
> —E. 846-850.

Hesiod's description of the contest, which has been
justly held to constitute his title to a rank near Homer
as an epic poet, is prefaced by a feast at which Zeus
addresses his allies, and receives in turn the assurance
of their support. The speeches are not wanting in
dignity, though briefer than those which, in his great
epic, Milton has moulded on their model. Our English poet had bathed his spirit in Hesiod before he
essayed the sixth book of his 'Paradise Lost;' and it
was well and wisely done by the translator of the following description of the war betwixt Zeus and the
Titans to aim at a Miltonic style and speech:—

> "All on that day roused infinite the war,
> Female and male; the Titan deities,
> The gods from Cronus sprang, and those whom Zeus
> From subterranean gloom released to light:
> Terrible, strong, of force enormous; burst
> A hundred arms from all their shoulders huge:
> From all their shoulders fifty heads upsprang
> O'er limbs of sinewy mould. They then arrayed
> Against the Titans in fell combat stood,
> And in their nervous grasp wielded aloft
> Precipitous rocks. On the other side alert

> The Titan phalanx closed: then hands of strength
> Joined prowess, and displayed the works of war.
> Tremendous then the immeasurable sea
> Roared : earth resounded : the wide heaven throughout
> Groaned shattering: from its base Olympus vast
> Reeled to the violence of the gods: the shock
> Of deep concussion rocked the dark abyss
> Remote of Tartarus : the shrilling din
> Of hollow tramplings and strong battle-strokes,
> And measureless uproar of wild pursuit.
> So they reciprocal their weapons hurled
> Groan-scattering, and the shout of either host
> Burst in exhorting ardour to the stars
> Of heaven : with mighty war-cries either host
> Encountering closed."
> —E. 683-908.

A pause at this point may be excused, seeing that it affords the opportunity of noting the contrast between the heathen and the Christian conceptions of divine strength. In Milton the Messiah has a superabundance of might :—

> " Yet half his strength he put not forth, but checked
> His thunder in mid volley, for he meant
> Not to destroy, but root them out of heaven."
> —Par. Lost, vi. 853-855.

In the conflict with the Titans, Zeus has to exert all his might to insure victory :—

> " Nor longer then did Zeus
> Curb his full power, but instant in his soul
> There grew dilated strength, and it was filled
> With his omnipotence. *At once he loosed*
> *His whole of might, and put forth all the god.*

The vaulted sky, the mount Olympian flashed
With his continu'd presence, for he passed
Incessant forth, and scattered fires on fires.
Hurled from his hardy grasp the lightnings flew
Reiterated swift; the whirling flash
Cast sacred splendour, and the thunderbolt
Fell: roared around the nurture-yielding earth
In conflagration; for on every side
The immensity of forests crackling blazed:
Yea, the broad earth burned red, the streams that mix
With ocean and the deserts of the sea.
Round and around the Titan brood of earth
Rolled the hot vapour on its fiery surge.
The liquid heat air's pure expanse divine
Suffused: the radiance keen of quivering flame
That shot from writhen lightnings, each dim orb,
Strong though they were, intolerable smote,
And scorched their blasted vision: through the void
Of Erebus the preternatural glare
Spread mingling fire with darkness. But to see
With human eye and hear with the ear of man
Had been as if midway the spacious heaven
Hurtling with earth shocked—e'en as nether earth
Crashed from the centre, and the wreck of heaven
Fell ruinous from high. So vast the din
When, gods encountering gods, the clang of arms
Commingled, and the tumult roared from heaven."
—E. 908-939.

To heighten the turmoil, the winds and elements fight on the side of Zeus. The tide of battle turns. Jove's huge auxiliaries overwhelm the Titans with a succession of great missiles, send them sheer beneath the earth, and consign them to a durance " as far beneath, under earth, as heaven is from earth, for equal is the space from earth to murky Tartarus." There, in the deeper chamber of an abyss from which there is no escape, the Titans are thenceforth imprisoned, with the hundred-handed giants set over them as keepers, and with Day and Night acting as sentries or janitors in front of the brazen threshold:—

> " There Night
> And Day, near passing, mutual greeting still
> Exchange, alternate as they glide athwart
> The brazen threshold vast. This enters, that
> Forth issues, nor the two can one abode
> At once constrain. This passes forth and roams
> The round of earth, that in the mansion waits
> Till the due season of her travel come.
> Lo! from the one the far-discerning light
> Beams upon earthly dwellers: but a cloud
> Of pitchy darkness veils the other round:
> Pernicious Night, aye leading in her hand
> Sleep, Death's twin brother: sons of gloomy Night,
> There hold they habitation, Death and Sleep,
> Dread deities: nor them doth shining sun
> E'er with his beam contemplate, when he climbs
> The cope of heaven, or when from heaven descends.
> Of these the one glides gentle o'er the space
> Of earth and broad expanse of ocean waves,
> Placid to man. The other has a heart
> Of iron: yea, the heart within his breast
> Is brass unpitying: whom of men he grasps,
> Stern he retains: e'en to immortal gods
> A foe." —E. 992-1014.

Of these sentries the readers of Milton's ' Paradise Lost' may recall the description at the opening of the sixth book; whilst the counterparts of the twin chil-

dren of Night may be found in the Iliad,* as well as
in the Æneid.†

Another wonder of the prison-house, in Hesiod's
account of it, is Cerberus:—

> "A grisly dog, implacable,
> Watching before the gates. A stratagem
> Is his, malicious: them who enter there,
> With tail and bended ears he fawning soothes,
> But suffers not that they with backward step
> Repass: whoe'er would issue from the gates
> Of Pluto strong and stern Persephone,
> For them with marking eye he lurks: on them
> Springs from his couch, and pitiless devours."
> —E. 1018-1026.

In close proximity to this monster was the fabled
Styx, in some respects the most awful personage in
the 'Theogony.' The legend about her is somewhat
obscure, but it is curious as being connected with that
of Iris, the rainbow, whose function of carrying up
water when any god has been guilty of falsehood
seems a vague embodiment of the covenant sealed by
the "bow set in the cloud:"—

> "Jove sends Iris down
> To bring the great oath in a golden ewer,
> The far-famed water, from steep, sky-capt rock
> Distilling in cold stream. Beneath the earth
> Abundant from the sacred river-head
> Through shades of darkest night the Stygian horn
> Of Ocean flows: a tenth of all the streams
> To the dread Oath allotted. In nine streams
> Circling the round of earth and the broad seas

* Il. xiv. 231, &c. † Æn. vi. 278, &c.

With silver whirlpools twined with many a maze,
It falls into the deep: one stream alone
Glides from the rock, a mighty bane to gods.
Who of immortals, that inhabit still
Olympus topped with snow, libation pours
And is forsworn, he one whole year entire
Lies reft of breath, nor yet approaches once
The nectared and ambrosial sweet repast:
But still reclines on the spread festive couch
Mute, breathless: and a mortal lethargy
O'erwhelms him; but his malady absolved
With the great round of the revolving year,
More ills on ills afflictive seize: nine years
From everlasting deities remote
His lot is cast: in council nor in feast
Once joins he, till nine years entire are full.
. . . .
So great an oath the deities of heaven
Decreed the waters incorruptible,
Ancient, of Styx, who sweeps with wandering wave
A rugged region: where of dusky Earth,
And darksome Tartarus, and Ocean waste,
And the starred Heaven, the source and boundary
Successive rise and end: a dreary wild
And ghastly, e'en by deities abhorred."
—E. 1038-1072.

Such, according to Hesiod, are the surroundings of
the infernal prison-house which received the vanquished
Titans when Jove's victory was assured. Not yet, however, could he rest from his toil: he had yet to scotch
the half-serpent, half-human Typhœus, the offspring of
a new union betwixt Earth and Tartarus,—a monster so
terror-inspiring by means of its hundred heads and voices
to match, that Olympus might well dread another and

less welcome master should this pest attain full devel
opment. Zeus, we are told, foresaw the danger:—

" Intuitive and vigilant and strong
He thundered: instantaneous all around
Earth reeled with horrible crash: the firmament
Roared of high heaven, the ocean streams and seas,
And uttermost caverns! *While the king in wrath
Uprose, beneath his everlasting feet
Trembled Olympus: groaned the steadfast earth.*
From either side a burning radiance caught
The darkly-rolling ocean, from the flash
Of lightnings and the monster's darted flame,
Hot thunderbolts, and blasts of fiery winds.
Glowed earth, air, sea: the billows heaved on high
Foamed round the shores, and dashed on every side
Beneath the rush of gods. Concussion wild
And unappeasable arose: aghast
The gloomy monarch of th' infernal dead
Trembled: the sub-Tartarean Titans heard
E'en where they stood and Cronus in the midst;
They heard appalled the unextinguished rage
Of tumult and the din of dreadful war.
Now when the god, the fulness of his might
Gathering at once, had grasped his radiant arms,
The glowing thunderbolt and bickering flame,
He from the summit of th' Olympian mount
Leapt at a bound, and smote him: hissed at once
The horrible monster's heads enormous, scorched
In one conflagrant blaze. When thus the god
Had quelled him, thunder-smitten, mangled, prone,
He fell: beneath his weight earth groaning shook.
Flame from the lightning-stricken prodigy
Flashed 'mid the mountain hollows, rugged, dark,
Where he fell smitten. Broad earth glowed intense
From that unbounded vapour, and dissolved:—

As fusile tin, by art of youths, above
The wide-brimmed vase up-bubbling, foams with heat ;
Or iron hardest of the mine, subdued
By burning flame, amid the mountain dells
Melts in the sacred caves beneath the hands
Of Vulcan,—so earth melted in the glare
Of blazing fire. He down wide Hell's abyss
His victim hurled, in bitterness of soul."
—E. 1108-1149.

The italicised lines may recall the noble image in the 'Paradise Lost ;'* a passage which Milton's editor, Todd, pronounces grander in conception than Hesiod's. But, as Elton fairly answers, it is only in Milton's reservation that he is superior. "The mere rising of Zeus causing mountains to rock beneath his everlasting feet, is sublimer than the firmament shaking from the rolling of wheels."

After quelling this monster, Zeus is represented bethinking himself of a suitable consort, and espousing Metis or Wisdom, so as to effect a union of absolute wisdom with absolute power. As, however, in the Hesiodic view of the divinity, there was ever a risk of dethronement to the sire at the hand of his offspring, Zeus hit upon a plan which should prevent his wife producing a progeny that might hereafter conspire with her to dethrone him, after the hereditary fashion. He absorbed Metis, with her babe yet unborn, in his own breast, and, according to mythology, found this task

* " Under his burning wheels
The steadfast empyrean shook throughout,
All but the throne itself of God."
—vi. 832-834.

easier through having persuaded her to assume the most diminutive of shapes. Thenceforth he blended perfect wisdom in his own body, and in due time, as from a second womb—

> "He from his head disclosed, himself, to birth
> The blue-eyed maid Tritonian Pallas, fierce,
> Rousing the war-field's tumult, unsubdued,
> Leader of armies, awful, whose delight
> The shout of battle and the shock of war."
> —E. 1213-1217.

Yet, notwithstanding so summary a putting away of his first wife, Zeus, it appears, had no mind to remain a widower. Themis bare him the Hours; Eurynome the Graces—

> "Whose eyelids, as they gaze,
> Drop love unnerving; and beneath the shade
> Of their arched brows they steal the sidelong glance
> Of sweetness;"
> —E. 1196-1199.

and Mnemosyne, a daughter of Uranus, became the mother by him of the Nine Muses, celebrated by Hesiod at the beginning of the poem. With Demeter and Latona also he had tender relations, before he finally resigned himself to his sister Hera (Juno), who took permanent rank as Queen of the Gods. From this union sprang Mars and Hebe, and Eileithyia or Lucina: whilst according to Hesiod, who herein differs from Homer, Hephæstus or Vulcan was the offspring of Hera alone, as a set-off to Zeus's sole parentage of Athena. Of the more illicit amours of the fickle king of the gods, and of their issues, and

the marriages consequent upon these children of the gods
espousing nymphs or mortals. Hesiod has still much
to tell, in his fashion of genealogising, before we reach
the Heroogony, or list of heroes born of the union of
goddesses with mortal men, which is tacked to the 'Theogony' proper, as it has come down to us. It is indeed
a list and little more; tracing, for example, the birth of
Plutus to the meeting of Demeter with Iasius in the
wheat-fields of Crete; of Achilles, to the union of Peleus
with Thetis; of Latinus, Telegonus, and another, to the
dalliance of Ulysses with the divine Circe.

"Lo! these were they who, yielding to embrace
 Of mortal men, themselves immortal, gave
 A race resembling gods."
—E. 1324-1236.

Thus virtually ends the 'Theogony' in its extant
form, but our sketch of it would not be complete were
we to ignore the story of Pandora and Prometheus,
which has been passed over at its proper place in the
genealogy, with a view to a clearer unfolding of the
sequence of the poem. In the 'Works' this legend
is an episode; in the 'Theogony' it is a piece of genealogy, *à propos* of the offspring of Iapetus, the brother
of Cronus, and Clymene. Atlas, one of their sons, was
doomed by Zeus to bear up the vault of heaven as an
eternal penalty; Menœtius, another, was for his inso-
lence thrust down to Erebus by the lightning-flash.
Of Epimetheus, who in the 'Works' accepts the gift
of Pandora, it is simply said in the 'Theogony' that
he did so, and brought evil upon man by his act.
Nothing is said of heedlessness of his brother's cau-

tion; nothing of the casket of evils, from which in the
'Works,' Pandora, by lifting the lid, lets mischief
and disease loose upon the world. The key to the
difference between the two accounts is to be found
in the fact that in the 'Works' Hesiod narrates the
consequences of the sin of Prometheus; in the 'Theogony,' the story of the sin itself. In the order of
events that story would run thus: Prometheus enrages
Zeus by scoffing at sacrifices, and by tricking the sage
ruler of Olympus into a wrong choice touching the
most savoury part of the ox. In his office of arbitrator,
he divides two portions, the flesh and entrails covered
with the belly on one hand, the bones under a cover
of white fat on the other. Zeus chooses after the
outward appearance, but, as Hesiod seems to imply,
chooses wittingly, for the sake of having a grievance.
Thenceforth in sacrifice it was customary to offer the
whitening bones at his altars. But the god neither
forgot nor forgave the cheat—

> "And still the fraud remembering from that hour,
> The strength of unexhausted fire denied
> To all the dwellers upon earth. But him
> Benevolent Prometheus did beguile:
> The far-seen splendour in a hollow reed
> He stole of inexhaustible flame. But then
> Resentment stung the Thunderer's inmost soul,
> And his heart chafed with anger when he saw
> The fire far-gleaming in the midst of men.
> Straight for the flame bestowed devised he ill
> To man."
> —E. 749-759.

Outwitted twice, he roused himself to take vengeance

upon Prometheus as well as his clients. On the latter he inflicted the evil of winsome womankind, represented by Pandora, and placed them in the dilemma of either not marrying, and dying heirless, or of finding in marriage the lottery which it is still accounted. As to Prometheus and his punishment, Hesiod's account is as follows:—

> "Prometheus, versed
> In various wiles, he bound with fettering chains
> Indissoluble, chains of galling weight,
> Midway a column. Down he sent from high
> The broad-winged eagle: she his liver gorged
> Immortal. For it sprang with life, and grew
> In the night season, and the waste repaired
> Of what by day the bird of spreading wing
> Devoured."
> —E. 696-704.

This durance was eventually terminated by Hercules slaying the vulture or eagle, and reconciling Zeus and the Titan. Hesiod's moral will sum up the tale:—

> "Nathless it is not given thee to deceive
> The god, nor yet elude the omniscient mind;
> For not Prometheus, void of blame to man,
> Could 'scape the burden of oppressive wrath;
> And vain his various wisdom; vain to free
> From pangs, or burst the inextricable chain."
> —E. 816-821.

The foregoing sketch will, it is hoped, have enabled English readers to discover in Hesiod's 'Theogony' not a mere prosy catalogue, but a systematised account of the generation of the gods of Hellas, relieved of excessive detail by fervid descriptions, stirring battle-pieces, noble images, and graceful fancies. Such as it was, it appears to have found extensive circulation and acceptance in Greece, and to have formed the chief source of information amongst Greeks concerning the divine antiquity. This is not the kind of work to admit of a comparison of the so-called Orphic Theogony, which, in point of fact, belongs to a much later date, with that of Hesiod. Enough to state that the former, to use Mr Grote's expression, "contains the Hesiodic ideas and persons, enlarged and mystically disguised." But those who have the time and materials for carrying out the comparison for themselves, will be led to discover in the development of religious belief, in the bias towards a sort of unity of Godhead, and in the investment of the powers of nature with the attributes of deity, which characterise the Orphic worship and theogonies, indirect corroboration of the opinion which assigns a very early date to the simple, unmystical, and, so to speak, unspiritual view of the divine foretime, handed down to us in Hesiod's theogonic system.

CHAPTER V.

THE SHIELD OF HERCULES.

It was remarked at the outset that one class of Hesiodic poems consisted of epics *in petto* on some subject of heroic mythology. The 'Shield of Hercules' survives as a sample, if indeed it is to be received as Hesiod's work. Its theme is a single adventure of Hercules, his combat with Cycnus and his father, the war-god, near Apollo's Temple at Pagasæ. Shorn of a preface of fifty-six verses borrowed from the 'Catalogue of Women,' and having for their burden the artifice of Zeus with Alcmena, which resulted in the birth of Hercules, a preface manifestly in the wrong place, the 'Shield' is a fairly compact poem, constructed as a frame for the description of the hero's buckler, to which the rest of the poem is ancillary. Among the ancients the balance of opinion leaned to the belief that it was written by the author of the 'Theogony;' but though there is insufficient ground for the wholesale depreciation cast upon it by Mure, in his 'History of the Language and Literature of Ancient Greece,' it can hardly be maintained that the 'Shield of Hercules' is a poem of the same age and authorship as the 'Works' or the 'Theogony.' The sounder criticism of Müller deems it worthy to be set side by side with Homer's account of the Shield of Achilles in the 13th book of the Iliad, and characterises it as executed in the genuine spirit of the Hesiodian school. Were it desirable, it might be shown from the writings of the same critic* that the objects represented on Hesiod's shield were in fact the first subjects of the Greek artificers in bronze, and that there are proofs in the accoutrement of Hercules, not with club and lion's skin, but like other heroes, of a date for this poem not posterior to the 40th Olympiad.

It has, no doubt, been the ill-fortune of this poem to have attracted more than its fair share of botchers and interpolators, and the discrimination of the true gold from the counterfeit and base metal belongs rather to a critical edition of the Hesiodic remains; but in the glance which we propose to bestow upon the work as it has come down to us, it will be shown that, after considerable allowance for interpolated passages, a residuum of fine heroic poetry will survive the process.

The poem proper, it has been said, begins at v. 57. Hercules, on reaching manhood, had undertaken an expedition against a noted robber, Cycnus, the son of Ares and Pelopia. This Cycnus used to infest the mountain-passes between Thessaly and Boeotia, and sacrilegiously waylay the processions to Delphi. It seems he would have been willing to buy off Apollo's

* Hist. Gr. Lit., i. 132.

wrath by building him at Pagasæ an altar of the horns of captured beasts; but the god loved his shrine too well to compound matters so easily, and instead of doing so, appears to have commissioned Hercules to exact reparation from the robber. The poem opens with the approach of the hero, with his charioteer and kinsman, Iolaus, to the robber's haunt:—

" There in the grove of the far-darting god
He found him, and, insatiable of war,
Ares, his sire, beside. Both bright in arms,
Bright in the sheen of burning flame they stood
On their high chariot, and the horses fleet
Trampled the ground with rending hoofs; around
In parted circle smoked the cloudy dust,
Up-dashed beneath the trampling hoofs, and cars
Of complicated frame. The well-framed cars
Rattled aloud; loud clashed the wheels, while wrapt
In their full speed the horses flew. Rejoiced
The noble Cycnus; for the hope was his
Jove's warlike offspring and his charioteer
To slay, and strip them of their gorgeous mail.
But to his vaunts the prophet god of day
Turned a deaf ear: for he himself set on
The assault of Heracles."
—E. 81-97.

None but Hercules, we are told, could have faced the unearthly light with which the sheen of the wargod's armour and the glare of his fire-flashing eyes lit up the sacred enclosure and its environs. He, however, is equal to the occasion. Probably, if we had the poem as it was written, the hero would not be represented as in the text, employing this critical moment in irrelevant speeches to his charioteer to the effect that the labours (in which, by the way, his soul delighted) were all occasioned by the folly of that charioteer's father, Iphiclus. It was an odd time to twit his comrade and his brother's son with that brother's errors, when a fight with Ares, the god of war, was imminent. Iolaus's answer is more to the point. He bids his chief rely on Zeus and Poseidon for victory in the encounter, and urges him to don his armour in readiness for a fray in which the race of Alcaeus, to which Hercules *putatively* belongs, shall get the victory:—

"He said, and Hercules smiled stern his joy,
Elate of thought: for he had spoken words
Most welcome. Then in winged accents thus:
'Jove-fostered hero, it is e'en at hand,
The battle's rough encounter: thou, as erst,
In martial prudence firm, aright, aleft,
With vantage of the fray unerring guide
Areion, huge and sable-maned; and me
Aid in the doubtful conflict, as thou may'st.'"
— E. 157-165.

It would appear that the horse here mentioned owes its prominence to being of divine strain, and the offspring of the sea-god. The other member of the pair is not named, because of the transcendent breed of its yoke-fellow, who is, in the twenty-third book of the Iliad, said to belong to Adrastus.

But now the hero begins his war-toilet, donning his greaves of mountain-brass, the corselet which is Athena's gift, and the sword from the same donor, which he slings athwart his shoulders. Of the arrows in his quiver the poet says

THE SHIELD OF HERCULES.

> " Shuddering horrors these
> Inflicted, and the agony of death
> Sudden, that chokes the suffocative voice;
> The points were barbed with death and bitter-steeped
> With human tears: burnished the length'ning shafts,
> And they were feathered from the tawny plume
> Of eagles."
>   —E. 177-183.

The heroic spear and helm complete his equipment, save and except the shield, to which it has been above noted that all the rest is introductory. This would seem to have been a circular disc, with a dragon for centre, and the parts between it and the outer rim divided by layers of cyanus or blue steel into four compartments of enamel, ivory, electrum, and gold. According to Müller,* a battle of wild boars and lions forms a narrow band round the middle. The first considerable band which surrounds the centre-piece in the circle consists of four departments, of which two contain warlike, and two peaceable subjects, so that the entire shield contains, as it were, a sanguinary and a tranquil side. The rim of the shield is surrounded by the ocean. An idea of the poem is best gathered from some of the details of the several parts. Perched in the centre on the dragon's head—

> " Stern Strife in air
> Hung hovering, and arrayed the war of men;
> Haggard; whose aspect from all mortals reft
> All mind and soul; whoe'er in brunt of arms
> Should match their strength, and face the son of Zeus,
> Below this earth their spirits to the abyss

* Hist. Gr. Lit., i. 132.

Descend; and through the flesh that wastes away
Beneath the parching Sun, their whitening bones
Start forth and moulder in the sable dust."
—E. 200-208.

Around this central image are grouped the appropriate forms of " Rout," " Rallying," " Terror," " Tumult," " Carnage," and " Discord ;" but in close proximity to the dragon's head came twelve serpent-heads, freezing with dread all mortal combatants, and endowed, it should seem, with properties not inherent in the metal of the shield. The translation is as follows:—

"Oft as he
Moved to the battle, *from their clashing fangs
A sound was heard.* Such miracles displayed
The buckler's field with living blazonry
Resplendent ; and those fearful snakes were streaked
O'er their cerulean backs with streaks of jet,
And their jaws blackened with a jetty dye."
—E. 224-230.

But the original seems to imply that the rows of teeth, with which each serpent was finished, actually gnashed and clashed while Hercules was fighting. This, as Mr Paley suggests, may have been a mechanical device like that in the Theban Shields mentioned in the 'Phœnissæ' of Euripides, v. 11-26; or a bit of the marvellous—a "Munchausenism," such as ancient poets affect in enhancing the wonder of some work of the gods. Whichever it was, a like demand on our credulity is made in two other passages: one, where in another compartment Perseus is represented as seeming to hover over the shield's surface, like a man flying low in air, and to flit like a thought; —

> "There was the knight, of fair-haired Danae born,
> Perseus, nor yet the buckler with his feet
> Touched, nor yet distant hovered: strange to think;
> For nowhere on the surface of the shield
> He rested: so the crippled artist god,
> Illustrious, framed him with his hands in gold."
> —E. 297-302.

The other is where the noise of the Gorgons' feet, as they tread, is represented as realised in connection with the sculptured shield:—

> "Close behind the Gorgons twain
> Of nameless terror, unapproachable,
> Came rushing: eagerly they stretched their arms
> To seize him: from the pallid adamant
> Audibly as they rushed, the clattering shield
> Clanked with a sharp shrill sound."
> —E. 314-319.

Next to the serpent-heads on the shield was wrought a fight betwixt boars and lions—an occasion to the poet of spirited description:—

> "Wild from the forest, herds of boars were there,
> And lions, mutual glaring: these in wrath
> Leaped on each other; and by troops they drove
> Their onset: nor yet these nor those recoiled,
> Nor quaked in fear: of both the backs uprose,
> Bristling with anger: for a lion huge
> Lay stretched amidst them, and two boars beside,
> Lifeless: the sable blood down-dropping oozed
> Into the ground. So these with bowed backs
> Lay dead beneath the terrible lions; they
> For this the more incensed, both savage boars
> And tawny lions, chafing sprang to war."
> —E. 231-242.

Next came the battle of the Lapiths and Centaurs, the names of both races corresponding in the main with those in the first book of the Iliad. Both bands are wrought in silver, their arms and missiles in gold. The Centaurs, it is noteworthy, have not yet assumed the double form of man and beast, of which the first mention occurs in Pindar (Pyth. ii. 80), but are here the rude monsters we find under the same name in the Iliad and Odyssey—a fact which is of some importance in fixing the comparatively early date of the shield. On the same compartment is wrought, the poet tells us, Ares in his war-chariot, attended by Fear and Consternation; whilst Pallas, taking the spoil, spear in hand, with helmed brow and her ægis athwart her shoulders, is depicted as she sets the battle in array, and rushes forth to mingle in the war din.

After a description following next of the material wealth of Olympus, which has been suspected of spuriousness, as savouring of post-Homeric style and ideas, occurs a curious presentment of a harbour and surging sea, wrought of tin, in which silver dolphins are chasing the lesser fish, and amusing themselves with gorging these, and spouting up water, whale fashion. The little fish are wrought in brass. A later addition to the picture is obviously interpolated from Theocritus (i. 39), namely, the fisherman on a crag—

"Observant, in his grasp who held a net,
Like one that poising rises to the throw."

What is needed to complete the picture in the Alexandrian poet is, however, *de trop* here.

The description of Perseus, and his encounter with the Gorgons, has been partially anticipated, though our citations did not include the Gorgon's head covering all his back, his silver knapsack with gold tassels, or his invisible cap, the "helmet of Hades," which occurs in the fifth book of the Iliad, and has passed into a proverb. Above this group were wrought two cities, one at war, the other at peace. The details of the former are lifelike; able-bodied men engaged in fight, women beating their breasts upon the walls, the elders at the gates asking help of the blessed gods; whilst the Fates with interest survey and fan the work of siege and slaughter with a prospect to a coming banquet of blood :—

> " Hard by there stood
> Clotho, and Lachesis, and Atropos
> Somewhat in *years* inferior : nor was she
> A mighty goddess ; yet those other Fates
> Exceeding, and of birth the elder far."
> —E. 346-350.

Had the translator read *size* for years, Hesiod's account would have tallied with the evidence of vases and terra-cottas, which represent Clotho as the tallest, and Atropos the most decrepit of the weird sisters. Appropriately near this group is seen—

> " Misery, wan and ghastly, worn with woe,
> Arid and *swoln of knee*, with hunger's pains
> Faint falling : from her lean hands long the nails
> Outgrew : an ichor from her nostrils flowed.
> Blood from her cheeks distilled to earth : with teeth
> All wide, disclosed in grinning agony

> She stood : a cloud of dust her shoulders spread,
> And her eyes ran with tears"
>
> —E. 355-362.

The italicised words in the above description recall a curious image of starvation, " pressing a tumid foot with hand from hunger lean," in the 'Works and Days' (v. 692), and to some extent point to a kindred authorship of the two poems.

From this ghastly picture the poet soon carries his readers to a contrast on the same band of the shield—a city at peace, which has been supposed to be meant for Thebes. We recognise the towers and the seven gates, and become spectators of bridal processions to the sound of the flute, as opposed as possible to the revels of the war-god in that city in its day of trouble—revels which Euripides described as " most unmusical." Here is some account of what is passing :—

> "Some on the smooth-wheeled car
> A virgin bride conducted : then burst forth
> Aloud the marriage song, and far and wide
> Loud splendours flashed from many a quivering torch,
> Borne in the hands of slaves. Gay blooming girls
> Preceded ; and the dancers followed blithe.
> These with shrill pipe indenting the soft lip
> Breathed melody, while broken echoes thrilled
> Around them : to the lyre with flying touch,
> Those led the love-enkindling dance. A group
> Of youths was elsewhere imaged ; to the flute
> Disporting, some in dances and in song,
> In laughter others. To the minstrel's pipe
> So passed they on, and the whole city seemed
> As filled with pomps, with dances, and with feasts."
>
> —E. 366-380.

A comparison of this passage with its parallel in Homer's shield of Achilles (Il. xviii.), encourages the theory that both poets had a common ideal, though the representation is more full and prolix in Hesiod. We quote the Homeric description from an unpublished translation : *—

 "Two cities of mankind he wrought. In one
 Marriage was made and revelry went on.
 Here brides environed with bright torches' blaze
 Forth from their bowers they lead, and loudly raise
 The nuptial chant ; and dancers blithely spring,
 Cheered by the sweet-breathed pipe and harper's string,
 And women at their doors stand wondering."

A distinct subject, having nothing to do with the nuptial procession, though perhaps an accessory illustration of a city at peace, is formed in the operations of husbandry ; ploughers *tucked up* and *close girt* are making the furrow, as on the Homeric shield, yield before the coulter. The equipment of these ploughmen carries us back again to the 'Works,' where the husbandman is advised "to sow stripped, plough stripped, and reap stripped," if he would enjoy the gift of Ceres; and where "stripping" means probably getting rid of the cloak, and wearing only the close tunic :—

 "Next arose
 A field thick set with depth of corn : where some
 With sharpened sickle reaped the club-like stalks,
 Some bound them into bands, and strewed the floor
 For thrashing."—E.

* By Mr Richard Garnett.

And in close proximity was the delineation of a vintage: some gathering the fruit, vine-sickle in hand, and others carrying it away in baskets. By a marvellous skill in metals, a row of vines had been wrought in gold, waving with leaves and trellises of silver, and bending with grapes represented in some dark metal. Treading the winepress, and expressing the juice, completed the picture, which is less perfect than Homer's parallel passage.

But there was room found, it would seem, on this part of the shield, for athletic and field sports of various kinds, the chariot-race being the most elaborate description of the set :—

"High o'er the well-compacted chariots hung
The charioteers : the rapid horses loosed
At their full stretch, and shook the floating reins.
Rebounding from the ground with many a shock
Flew clattering the firm cars, and creaked aloud
The naves of the round wheels. They therefore toiled
Endless : nor conquest yet at any time
Achieved they, but a doubtful strife maintained."
—E. 413-420.

Around the shield's verge was represented the circumambient ocean, girdling, as it did in Homer's view, the flat and circular earth with its boundless flood :—

"Rounding the utmost verge the ocean flowed
As in full swell of waters : and the shield
All variegated with whole circle bound.
Swans of high-hovering wing there clamoured shrill,
Who also skimmed the breasted surge with plume
Innumerous : near them fishes 'midst the waves
Frolicked in wanton leaps,"–
E. 424-429.

so like the life, the poet adds, as to exact the admiration of even Zeus, the artificer's sire and patron.

So much for the shield: what remains concerns the combat betwixt Hercules and Cycnus with the war-god to help him. The odds are partially balanced by the aid of the blue-eyed Pallas to the hero, who by her counsel forbears to dream of "spoiling the steeds and glorious armour of a god," a thing which he finds is against the decrees of fate. Nor does the goddess stop at advice, but vouchsafes her invisible presence in the hero's car. As the combatants come to close quarters Hercules resorts to mock civilities, and with taunting allusions asks free passage to the court of Ceyx, king of Iolchos, the father-in-law of Cycnus. As a matter of course the permission is denied. Hercules and Cycnus leap to the ground, and their charioteers drive a little aside to give free scope for the tug of war:—

"As rocks
From some high mountain-top precipitate
Leap with a bound, and o'er each other whirled
Shock in the dizzying fall; and many an oak
Of lofty branch, pine-tree, and poplar, deep
Of root, are crashed beneath them; as their course
Rapidly rolls, till now they reach the plain;
So met these foes encountering, and so burst
Their mighty clamour. Echoing loud throughout
The city of the Myrmidons gave back
Their lifted voices, and Iolchos famed,
And Arnê, and Anthea's grass girt walls,
And Helicê. Thus with amazing shout
They joined in battle: all-consulting Zeus
Then greatly thundered: from the clouds of heaven

He cast forth dews of blood, and signal thus
Of onset gave to his high-daring son."
—E. 506-522.

The simile of the dislodged rocks reminds us of
Hector's onslaught in the thirteenth book of the
Iliad; but the poetical figure of the cities re-echoing
the din and clamour of the conflict, and the portent of
the bloody rain-drops, are due to Hesiod's own ima-
gination. Close following upon these comes a tissue
of similes, so prodigally strewn that they strike the
critical as later interpolations. The issue of the fight
is conceived in a more genuine strain :—

"Truly then
Cycnus, the son of Zeus unmatched in strength
Aiming to slay, against the buckler struck
His brazen lance, but through the metal plate
Broke not. The present of a god preserved.
On the other side, he of Amphitryon named,
Strong Heracles, between the helm and shield
Drave his long spear, and, underneath the chin
Through the bare neck smote violent and swift.
The murderous ashen beam at once the nerves
Twain of the neck cleft sheer: for all the man
Dropped, and his force went from him: down he fell
Headlong. As falls a thunder-blasted oak,
Or perpendicular rock, riven with the flash
Of Zeus, in smouldering smoke is hurled from high,
So fell he."
—E. 558-573.

Hercules, so far victorious, awaits the onset of the
bereaved war-god with a devout heedfulness of his
assessor's injunctions. She from her seat at his side
interposes to apprise Ares that any attempt at revenge

or reprisals must involve a conflict with herself. But the god, sore at his bereavement, heeds not her word, and with violent effort hurls his brazen spear at the huge shield of his antagonist. In vain; for Pallas diverts the javelin's force. Ares rushes upon Hercules, and he, having watched his opportunity,—

> "Beneath the well-wrought shield the thigh exposed
> Wounded with all his strength, the thrusting rived
> The shield's large disk, and cleft it with his lance,
> And in the midway threw him to the earth
> Prostrate."
>
> —E. 624-628.

a curious *dénouement*, wherein an immortal is in bitter need of a *Deus ex machina*. The author of the 'Shield,' however, has provided for the contingency. Fear and Consternation had sat as helpers in the chariot of Cycnus, as Pallas in that of Hercules. They hurry the vanquished god into his car, and, lashing the steeds, transport him without more ado to Olympus. Here the poem should have ended; but a later chronicler seems to have felt, like many a modern novelist, that the minor *dramatis personæ* must be accounted for. And so we have a few lines about the victor spoiling Cycnus, whose obsequies were afterwards duly performed by his respectable father-in-law Ceyx at Iolchos. But the tomb erected over the brigand and fane-robber was not suffered to remain in honour. In requital for repeated sacrilege—

> "Anaurus foaming high with wintry rains
> Swept it from sight away. Apollo thus

Commanded: for that Cycnus ambushed spoiled
By violence the Delphic hecatombs."
—E. 681-654

Thus ends our sole sample extant of the short epics which antiquity attributes to Hesiod. With all its repetitions and interpolations, there is in it a residuum of genuine poetry which is happily rescued from the spoils of time. Even as a "fugitive ballad," which Mure has designated it, it is too good to be lost; and though we may not venture to attribute it confidently to Hesiod, the 'Shield' has its place in classical literature, if we can even accept it as "Hesiodian."

CHAPTER VI.

IMITATORS OF HESIOD.

Although it would be impossible to point to any direct imitation of Hesiod in poetry subsequent to Virgil's, and though even his is only imitation within certain conditions, it seems incumbent on us to notice briefly the influence, for the most part indirect and unconscious, which his poetry, especially his didactic poetry, has had upon later poets. Those shorter epic scraps, of which the 'Shield of Hercules' is a sample, have their modern presentment, if anywhere, in idyls and professed fragments; but the differences here betwixt the old and the new are so considerable as to make it unsafe to press the likeness. For the 'Theogony' we have one or two modern parallels, though it, too, has served rather for a mine into which Christian apologists might dig for relics of heathen mythology, than as a type to be reproduced at the risk of that endlessness which is associated with genealogies. But as regards Hesiod's 'Works and Days,' there can be no question that its form, and its union of practical teaching with charm of versification, possessed an attraction for subsequent generations of poets, and, having been more or less borrowed from and remodelled, according to the demands of their subjects, by the poetical grammarians of Alexandria, was handed over as an example to the Alexandrianising poets of Rome. "The 'Phænomena' of Aratus," writes Professor Conington, in his introduction to the 'Georgics' "found at least two distinguished translators: Lucretius and Manilius gave the form and colour of poetry to the truths of science; Virgil and Horace to the rules of art; and the rear is brought up by such poets as Gratius, Nemesianus, and Serenus Sammonicus." But the 'Phænomena' of Aratus, and its Roman parallel, the 'Astronomica' of Manilius, though conversant with a portion of the same topics as Hesiod's didactic poem, essay a loftier flight of admonitory poetry; and in them the advance of time has substituted for the simplicity and directness of Hesiod, rhetorical turns and artifices, and the efforts of picturesque description. It is the same with Ovid's contemporary, Gratius Faliscus, if we may judge of him by his fragmentary 'Cynegetica.' In carrying out his design of a didactic poem on the chase and its surroundings, he barters simplicity for a forced elevation of moral tone, and spoils the effect of his real insight into his subject by a fondness for sententious maxims "in season and out of season." Nemesianus, who wrote two centuries or more after Gratius, seems to have so completely made Virgil his model that the influence of Hesiod is imperceptible in his poetry, which is diffuse and laboured, and instinct with exag-

gerated imitation of the Augustan poets. On the
whole, it is only between Hesiod and Virgil that solid
ground for comparison exists; and such as institute
this comparison will be constrained to admit Mr
Conington's conclusion, that the 'Works and Days'
as distinctly stimulated Virgil's general conception
of the Georgics, as the Idyls of Theocritus that of
his Bucolics, or the Iliad and Odyssey that of his
Æneid. Uncertainty as to the extent of the frag-
mentariness of the model undoubtedly bars a confident
verdict upon the closeness of the copy. Propertius
may have had other and lost works of Hesiod in his
mind's eye when he addressed his great contemporary
as repeating in song the Ascræan sage's precepts on
vine-culture as well as corn-crops (iii. 26, v. 77). Yet
enough of direct imitation survives in the large portion
of the first book of the Georgics (wherein Virgil
treads common ground) to show that, with many
points of contrast, there are also many correspondences
between the old Bœotian bard and his smoother Roman
admirer; and that where Virgil *does* copy, his copying
is as unequivocal as it is instructive for a study of
finish and refinement. Each poet takes for his theme
the same "glorification of labour" which Dean Meri-
vale discerns as the chief aim of the Georgics, the
difference consisting in the homeliness of the manner
of the Greek poet and the high polish of that of the
Roman. Each also recognises the time of man's
innocency, when this labour was not yet the law
of his being; and the treatment by each of the
myth of a golden or Saturnian age is not an inappro-

priate ground on which to trace their likeness and
unlikeness. As Hesiod's passage was not quoted in
our second chapter, its citation will be forgiven here,
the version selected being that of Mr Elton:—

" When gods alike and mortals rose to birth,
   A golden race the immortals formed on earth
Of many-languaged men: they lived of old,
When Saturn reigned in heaven, an age of gold.
Like gods they lived, with calm untroubled mind,
Free from the toils and anguish of our kind.
Nor e'er decrepit age misshaped their frame,
The hand's, the foot's proportions still the same.
Strangers to ill, their lives in feasts flowed by:
Wealthy in flocks; dear to the blest on high:
Dying they sank in sleep, nor seemed to die.
*Theirs was each good; the life-sustaining soil
Yielded its copious fruits, unbribed by toil.
They with abundant goods 'midst quiet lands
All willing shared the gathering of their hands.*"
                                  —E. 147-162.

Virgil does not set himself to reproduce the myth of
the metallic ages of mankind; but having assuredly
the original of the passage just quoted before him,
has seen that certain features of it are available for
introduction into his account of Jove's ordinance of
labour. He dismisses, we shall observe, the realistic
allusions to the sickness, death, and decrepit old age,
which in the golden days were " conspicuous by their
absence," and of which Hesiod had made much. These
apparently only suggest to him a couple of lines, in
which mortal cares are made an incentive to work,
instead of a destiny to be succumbed to; and the death

of the body is transferred to the sluggish lethargy of nature. To quote a very recent translator of the Georgics, Mr R. D. Blackmore :—

"'Twas Jove who first made husbandry a plan,
And care a whetstone for the wit of man;
Nor suffered he his own domains *to lie
Asleep in cumbrous old-world lethargy.
Ere Jove, the acres owned no master swain,
None durst enclose nor even mark the plain;
The world was common, and the willing land
More frankly gave with no one to demand.*"
—Georg. i. 121-128.

In the same spirit Virgil, in the second book of the Georgics, idealises the serenity of a rural existence, when he says of him who lives it :—

" Whatever fruit the branches and the mead
Spontaneous bring, he gathers for his need."
— Georg. ii. 500.

It is the idea of this spontaneity of boon nature which he has caught from Hesiod, as worth transferring ; and the task is achieved with grace, and without encumbrance. In the description of the process of making a plough, Virgil appears to copy Hesiod more closely than in the above passage ; and if we may accept Dr Daubeny's translation of the passage in the Georgics, the accounts correspond with a nicety almost incredible, considering the interval between the two poets. The curved piece of wood (or *buris*) of Virgil; the eight-foot pole (*temo*) joined by pins to the *buris* (or *buuse*, as it is called in the south of France); the bent handle (*stiva*) and the wooden share (*dentale*),—have

116   HESIOD.

all their counterparts in the directions for making
this implement given by Hesiod;—and the learned
author of 'Lectures on Roman Husbandry' considers
that both the Bœotian and the Roman plough may be
identified with the little improved *Herault* plough, still
in use in the south of France.* The storm-piece of
the earlier poet, again, is obviously present to the
mind of the graphic improver of it in the Augustan
age; though, in place of one point, the latter makes at
least half-a-dozen, and works up out of his predecessor's
hints a masterpiece of elaborate description. It need
scarcely be remarked, for it must strike every reader of
these poets, whether at first hand or second, that Virgil
constructs his "natural calendar" upon the very model
of Hesiod's. He catches the little hints of his model
with reference to the bird-scarer who is to follow the
plough-track; about the necessity of stripping to plough
or sow; about timing ploughing and seed-time by
the setting of the Pleiads; and about divers other
matters of the same rural importance. To quit the
first book of the Georgics, we see Hesiod's influence
occasionally exerting itself in the third; for, *à propos*
of the sharp-toothed dog which Hesiod prescribes in
his 'Works and Days' (604, &c.), and would have
the farmer feed well, as a protection from the night-
prowling thief, we find a parallel in Virgil:†—

" Nor last, nor least, the dogs must have their place !
With fattening whey support that honest race:
Swift Spartan whelps, Molossian mastiffs bold :—
With these patrolling, fear not for the fold,

* Rom. Husb., 100-102.   † Georg. iii. 403-408.

Though nightly thieves and wolves would fain attack,
And fierce Iberians never spare thy back."
— Blackmore, 94, 95.

And a lover of Hesiod's simple muse would be struck again and again, in the perusal of the four Georgics, with expansions of some germ from the older poet, calculated to make him appreciate more thoroughly the genius of both the original and the imitator. The landmarks and framework, as it were, of both, are the risings and settings of stars, the migrations of birds, and so forth; and though with Hesiod it was simplicity and nature that prompted him to avail himself of these, it is no small compliment that Virgil saw their aptitude for transference, and turned what was so spontaneous and unstudied to the purposes of art and culture. It is no fault, by the way, of Virgil, that he has not reproduced more fully and faithfully Hesiod's catalogue of "Lucky and Unlucky Days," at the end of his poem. The original is obscure and ambiguous. Virgil has caught all the transmutable matter in his passage of the first Georgic.*

As has been already said, when we have done with Virgil the resemblances of his successors and imitators to Hesiod are very faint and indistinct. To pass to our own poetry, it is natural to inquire, Have we aught of a kindred character and scope, that can claim to be accounted in any degree akin to Hesiod's 'Works and Days'? It need hardly be said that there is not a shadow of resemblance between him and Darwin

* v. 276-286.

or Bloomfield, though we have somewhere seen their names, as poets, set in juxtaposition. He is their master as a poet; he is their superior in simplicity. He is essentially ancient; they are wholly and entirely modern in thought, form, and expression. The didactic style, no doubt, has lent Hesiod's form to many of the compositions of the Augustan period of English literature. "We have had," says Mr Conington, in his introduction to the Georgics, "Essays on Satire, Essays on unnatural Flights in Poetry, Essays on translated Verse, Essays on Criticism, Essays on Man, Arts of preserving Health, Arts of Dancing, and even Arts of Cookery; the Chase, the Fleece, and the Sugar-cane." But, with his usual clear-sightedness, the late Oxford Professor of Latin saw that all these have grasped simply the form, and let go the spirit, of their model. The real parallel is to be found between the Ascrean farmer-poet and the quaint shrewd "British Varro" of the sixteenth century--

"Who sometime made the points of husbandry"—

Thomas Tusser, gentleman: a worthy whose "five hundred points, as well for the champion or open country as for the woodland or several," are quite worth the study of individual readers, not to say of agricultural colleges; so much wisdom, wit, and sound sense do they bring together into verse, which is, in very many characteristics, truly Hesiodian.

Endowed with an ear for music and a taste for farming, a compound of the singing-man (of St Paul's and Norwich cathedrals) and of the Suffolk grazier, a liberally-educated scholar withal for his day, this Tusser possessed several qualifications for the rank of our "English Hesiod." But unlike, so far as we know, the father of didactic poetry, neither his farming nor his poetry brought him success or profit; and his own generation regarded him as one who, with "the gift of sharpening others by his advice of wit," combined an inaptitude to thrive in his own person. He was born in 1523, and died in 1580. His 'Five Hundred Points of Good Husbandry' was printed in 1557; and no one will gainsay, after perusal of them, the opinion that, in the words of Dr Thomas Warton,* "this old English Georgic has much more of the simplicity of Hesiod than of the elegance of Virgil." Homely, quaint, and full of observation, his matter is curiously akin to that of the old Bœotian, after a due allowance for the world's advance in age; while the manner and measures are Tusser's own, and notable, not indeed as bearing any resemblance to the Hesiodic hexameters, but for a facility and variety consistent with the author's musical attainments, which are demonstrated in his use—indeed it may be his invention—of more than one popular English metre.

Although Tusser was indebted to Eton and King's College for his education, we have no reason to suppose that he had such acquaintance with Hesiod as could have suggested the shape and scope of his poem. It is better to attribute the coincidence of form to the practical turn and homely bent of the muse of each. That there is such coincidence will

* History of English Poetry, iii. 298-310.

be patent to the most cursory reader: the arrangement by months and by seasons, the counsels as to thrift and good economy, the eye to a well-ordered house, ever and anon provoke comparison. Warton, indeed, by a slip of the pen, denies the English Hesiod the versatility which indulges in digressions and invocations, and avers that "Ceres and Pan are not once named" by Tusser. But in an introduction to his book may be found at once a refutation of this not very serious charge, and, what is perhaps more to the point, a profession of the author's purpose in the volume, which has entitled him to a place of honour among early English poets. He writes as follows:—

> "Though fence well kept is one good point,
> And tilth well done in season due;
> Yet needing salve, in time t' anoint,
> Is all in all, and needful true:
>   As for the rest,
>   Thus think I best,
> As friend doth guest,
> With hand in hand to lead thee forth
> To Ceres' camp, there to behold
> A thousand things as richly worth
> As any pearl is worthy gold."
>   —Mavor's Tusser, xiii.

In the body of the work, expressions, sentiments, and sage counsels again and again remind us of Hesiod's lectures to Perses. The lesson that "'tis ill sparing the liquor at the bottom of the cask" reappears in such stanzas as—

> "Son, think not thy money purse-bottom to burn,
> But keep it for profit to serve thine own turn:

> A fool and his money be soon at debate,
> Which after, with sorrow, repents him too late."
> —xxiii. 11.

> "Some spareth too late, and a number with him—
> The fool at the bottom, the wise at the brim:
> Who careth nor spareth till spent he hath all,
> Of bobbing, not robbing, be careful he shall."
> —xxviii. 34.

At the same time he commends, quite in Hesiod's style, a prudent avoidance of the law-courts:—

> "Leave princes' affairs undescanted on,
> And tend to such doings as stands thee upon.
> Fear God, and offend not the prince nor his laws,
> And keep thyself out of the magistrate's claws."
> —xxix. 39.

Quite in Hesiod's groove, too, is Tusser's opinion about borrowing and lending; and his adagial way of discouraging the claims of relations and connections to a share in our farm profits savours curiously of the counsel of the 'Works and Days:'—

> "Be pinched by lending for kiffe nor for kin,
> Nor also by spending, by such as come in:
> Nor put to thine hand betwixt bark and the tree,
> Lest through thine own folly so pinched thou be.
>
> As lending to neighbour in time of his need
> Wins love of thy neighbour, and credit doth breed:
> So never to crave, but to live of thine own,
> Brings comforts a thousand, to many unknown."
> —xxvii. 30, 31.

We have seen, too, how Hesiod makes a point of prescribing very strictly the stuff which a farmer may keep without detriment to his purse and garner, of cautioning against too many helps, and so forth. Tusser is a little in advance of the Boeotian farmer-poet as to the full complement of hinds and dairy-maids; but the spirit of the following stanza is in exact keeping with the tone of the elder bard :—

> "Delight not for pleasure two houses to keep,
> Lest charge above measure upon thee do creep;
> And Jankin and Jennykin cozen thee so,
> To make thee repent it ere year about go."
> —xxx. 45.

It might be shown by other quotations that Tusser, like Hesiod, attaches due importance to the performance of religious ceremonies, and inculcates in fitting language seasonable offerings of thankfulness to a bounteous Providence; that he upholds well-timed hospitality, and commends a principle of liberality towards man or beast, if they deserve it. Of course, too, even in his shrewd homeliness, he does not so entirely as Hesiod calculate his hospitalities and liberalities with a sole eye to getting a *quid pro quo*. But it is perhaps more to the purpose to cite a few additional stanzas of Tusser's "Advice to Husbandmen," according to the season or month, with a stray verse or two which, *mutatis mutandis*, may serve to show that the spirit of Tusser was in effect the same which animated Hesiod so many centuries before him. This quatrain from "December's Husbandry" is an obvious parallel, to begin with :—

> "Yokes, forks, and such other let bailiff spy out,
> And gather the same, as he walketh about;

And after, at leisure, let this be his hire,
To *beath* them and trim them at home by the fire."*
—lx. 9.

Here again, in "June's Husbandry," is good provision for hay-making and hauling:—

" Provide of thine own to have all things at hand,
Lest work and the workman unoccupied stand:
Love seldom to borrow, that thinkest to save,
For he that once lendeth twice looketh to have.

Let cart be well searched without and within,
Well clouted and greased, ere hay-time begin:
Thy hay being carried, though carter had sworn,
Cart's bottom well boarded is saving of corn."
—p. 163.

And here sound practical counsel (sadly neglected too often) for insuring a safe corn-harvest:—

" Make suër of reapers, get harvest in hand:
The corn that is ripe doth but shed as it stand.
Be thankful to God for His benefits sent,
And willing to save it by honest intent."
—p. 182.

One would have liked to be able to think that so sound a counsellor had made a better trade of farming than he seems to have done. His ideas of being himself *captain* of every muster of his hands (p. 169), of encouraging them by extra wages at time of stress, and indeed all his suggestive hints, are fresh and pertinent even at this latter day; and if Thomas Tusser were more read, he would not fail of being oftener quoted.

* To *beath* or *bath* is to set green wood by the heat of a fire.
—Norfolk and Suffolk Dialect.

How timely, for example, is this advice to the
farmer, which in a Christian land should find thorough
acceptance, no matter what may have been the
demands upon him of the ill-advised amongst his
labourers!—

> "Once ended the harvest, let none be beguiled;
> Please such as did help thee—man, woman, and child:
> Thus doing, with alway such help as they can,
> Thou winnest the praise of the labouring man."
> —p. 188.

But, to complete our parallel with Hesiod, Tusser
has his descriptions of the winds and planets; is alive
to the wisdom of the "farm and fruit of old," as well
as of the improved courses of husbandry in his own
day: and if he now and then strikes out paths which
have no parallel in Hesiod, even in such cases the
homeliness and *naïveté* of his counsel savours of the
ancient poet in whose footsteps he so distinctly treads.
Though the domestic fowl does not figure in the
'Works and Days,' and the domestic cat is equally
unmentioned by the Bœotian didactic poet, the following mention of them both by Tusser reminds us of his
practical economic views, and would not have been
deemed by him beneath the dignity of the subject,
had poultry and mousers asserted the importance in
old days which they now demand:—

> "To rear up much poultry and want the barn door
> Is nought for the poulter, and worse for the poor;
> So now to keep hogs, and to starve them for meat,
> Is as to keep dogs for to bawl in the street.

As cat, a good mouser, is needful in house,
Because for her commons she killeth the mouse;
So ravening curs, as a many do keep,
Makes master want meat, and his dog to kill sheep."
—p. 48, 49.

Dr Thomas Warton, indeed, was disposed to regard Tusser as the mere rude beginner of what Mason perfected in his 'English Garden;' but it is a reasonable matter of taste whether the latter work at all comes up to the former in aught save an elegance bordering on affectation; and certainly there is nothing in Mason to suggest the faintest comparison with Hesiod's didactic poem. Tusser's work is probably its closest parallel in all the intervening ages.

It remains to inquire whether Hesiod's 'Theogony' has found with posterity as close an imitator as the work on which we have been dwelling. But this question is easily answered in the negative. The attempts of the so-called Orphic poets—the most considerable of whom were Cercops, a Pythagorean, and Onomacritus, a contemporary of the Pisistratids—to improve on the elder theogonies and cosmogonies, can hardly be mentioned in this category, being more mystical than mythical, and in the nature of refinements and abstractions, higher than the Hesiodic chaos. Nor, though full of mythologic learning even to cumbrousness, can the five hymns of the Alexandrian Callimachus be said to have aught of resemblance to the venerable system of Greek theogonies, which owes its promulgation to the genius of Hesiod. Studied and laboured to a fault, the legends which he connects

with the subjects of each hymn in succession are
tricked out with poetic devices very alien to the more
direct muse of Hesiod; and though Callimachus professes to record the speeches of Zeus and Artemis, and
to divine the thoughts and feelings that animate the
Olympians, his readers cannot help feeling that he
lacks the "afflatus" in which Hesiod implicitly believed,
and which, though it suited the sceptical Lucian to
twit as assumed, and unattended by results, certainly
imparts an air of earnestness to his poetry.* Furthermore—and this is the plainest note of difference—the
hymns of Callimachus have little or no pretence to be
"genealogies,"—a form of poetry, to say the truth, not
sufficiently attractive to please an advanced stage of
literary cultivation, and a form, too, that lacks any
memorable imitation in Latin poetry. To glance at
our own poetic literature, the nearest approach to the
form and scope of the 'Theogony' is to be found, it
strikes us, in Drayton's 'Polyolbion,' a poem characterised by the same endeavour to systematise a vast
mass of information, and to genealogise, so to speak,
the British hills, and woods, and rivers, which are
personified in it.

Drayton, it cannot be denied, has infinitely more
fancy, and lightens the burden of his accumulated
detail by much greater liveliness and idealism; yet it
is impossible not to be struck also with his enumeration
of the streams and mountains of a given district, each
invested with a personality, each for the nonce regarded
as of kin to its fellow, as a singular revival of Hesiod's

* Dialogue between Lucian and Hesiod, i. 35.

method in his 'Theogony;' a revival, to judge from a passage in his first song, surely not undesigned:—

"Ye sacred bards, that to your harps' melodious strings
Sung the ancient heroes' deeds (the monuments of kings),
And in your dreadful verse engraved the prophecies,
The aged world's descents, and genealogies;
If as those Druids taught, which kept the British rites
And dwelt in darksome caves, there counselling with
    sprites
(But their opinion failed, by error led away,
As since clear truth hath showed to their posterity),
When these our souls by death our bodies do forsake,
They instantly again do other bodies take;
I could have wished your spirits redoubled in my breast,
To give my verse applause to time's eternal rest."
—Polyolb., Song i. 30-42.

Our theory of a conscious reference to Hesiod's 'Theogony' by Drayton depends on the fourth verse of this extract; but, independently of this, almost any page in the 'Polyolbion' would furnish one or more illustrations of genealogism curiously Hesiodic. We might cite the rivers of Monmouth, Brecon, and Glamorgan, in the fourth song, or the Herefordshire streams in the seventh; but lengthy citations are impossible, and short extracts will ill represent the likeness which a wider comparison would confirm. In Pope's "Windsor Forest," the enumeration of the "seaborn brothers" of Old Father Thames, from "winding Isis" to "silent Darent,"

"Who swell with tributary urns his flood,"

is indubitably a leaf out of Drayton's book, and so

indirectly a tribute to Hesiod. Darwin's 'Botanic Garden,' and the 'Loves of the Plants,' affect indeed the genesis of nymphs and sylphs, of gnomes and salamanders; but the fanciful parade of these, amidst a crowd of metaphors, tropes, and descriptions, has nothing in it to remind us of Hesiod's 'Theogony,' unless it be a more tedious minuteness, and an exaggerated affectation of allegoric system. In truth, however, Hesiod's 'Theogony' is a work of which this or that side may be susceptible of parallel, but to which, in its own kind, and taken as a whole, none like nor second has arisen.

The 'Shield' and the 'Fragments' are of too doubtful authorship to call for the reflected light of parallelism; and so our task of laying before the reader a sketch of the life, works, and after-influence of the Ascræan poet is completed.

THEOGNIS.

CHAPTER I.

THEOGNIS IN YOUTH AND PROSPERITY.

WITH the life of Hesiod politics have little or no connection; in that of Theognis we find them playing an essential inseparable part. And it is curious that the very feature which both poets have in common, their subjectivity, is that which introduces us to this point of contrast and token of the ancient world's advancement —namely, that whereas Hesiod's political status is so unimportant as to be overlooked even by himself, with Theognis it occupies more space in his elegies than his social relations or his religious opinions. In fact, his personal and political life are so intermixed, that the internal evidence as to both must be collected in one skein, and cannot be separately unwound, unless at the risk of missing somewhat of the interest of his remains, which consists chiefly in the personality of the poet.

It is true that later Greek writers regarded Theognis

as a teacher of wisdom and virtue, by means of detached maxims and apothegms in elegiac verse, and would probably have been loath to recognise any element in his poetry which was personal or limited to particular times and situations; yet it is now fully established that he was one of the same section of poets with Callinus, Tyrtaeus, Solon, and Phocyllides, all of whom availed themselves of a form of versification, the original function of which was probably to express mournful sentiments, to inspire their countrymen with their own feelings as to the stirring themes of war and patriotism, of politics, and of love. With Theognis it is clear that the elegy was a song or poem sung at banquets or symposia after the libation, and between the pauses of drinking, to the sound of the flute; and, furthermore, that it was addressed not as elsewhere to the company at large, but to a single guest. Many such elegies were composed by him to friends and boon-companions, as may be inferred from his remains, and from the tradition which survives, that he wrote an elegy to the Sicilian Megarians on their escape from the siege of their city by Gelon (183 B.C.); but owing to the partiality of a later age for the maxims and moral sentiments with which these elegies were interspersed, and which, as we learn from Xenophon and Isocrates, were used in their day for educational purposes, the shape in which the poetry of Theognis has come down to us is as unlike the original form and drift as a handbook of maxims from Shakespeare is unlike an undoctored and un-Bowdlerised play. Thanks to the German editor Welcker, and to

the ingenious "restitution" of Hookham Frere, the
original type of these poems has been approximately
realised, and we are able, in a great measure, to con-
nect the assorted links into a consistent and personal
autobiography. For the clearer apprehension of this, it
seems best to give a very brief sketch of the political
condition of the poet's country at the time he flourished,
and then to divide our notice of himself and his works
into three epochs, defined and marked out by circumstances which gravely influenced his career and tone of
thought.

The poet's fatherland, the Grecian, not Sicilian,
Megara, after asserting its independence of Corinth, of
which it had been a colony, fell under the sway of a
Doric nobility, which ruled it in right of descent and
of landed estates. But before the legislation of Solon,
Theagenes, the father-in-law of Gelon, had become
tyrant or despot of Megara, like Cypselus and Periander
at Corinth, by feigned adoption of the popular cause.
His ascendancy was about B.C. 630-600, and upon his
overthrow the aristocratic oligarchy again got the upper
hand for a brief space, until the commons rose against
them, and succeeded in establishing a democracy of
such anarchical tendency and character, that it was not
long ere the expelled nobles were reinstated. The
elegies of Theognis, who was born about 570 B.C., date
from about the beginning of the democratic rule, and,
as he belonged to the aristocracy, deplore the sufferings
of his party, and the spoliation of their temples and
dwellings by the poor, who no longer paid the interest
of their debts. Frequent reference will be found in

his poetry to violent democratic measures, such as the adoption of the periœci, or cultivators without political rights, into the sovereign community; and, as might be imagined, in the case of one who was of the best blood and oldest stock, he constantly uses the term "the good" as a synonym for "the nobles," whilst the "bad and base" is his habitual expression to denote "the commonalty." In his point of view nothing brave and honourable was to be looked for from the latter, whilst nothing that was not so could possibly attach to the former. This distinction is a key to the due interpretation of his more political poems, and it accounts for much that strikes the reader as a hurtful and inexpedient prejudice on the part of the poet. For some time he would appear to have striven to preserve a neutrality, for which, as was to be expected, he got no credit from either side; but at last, whilst he was absent on a sea voyage, the "bad rich" resorted to a confiscation of his ancestral property, with an eye to redistribution among the commons. From this time forward he is found engaged in constant communications with Cyrnus, a young noble, who was evidently looked to as the coming man and saviour of his party; but the conspiracy, long in brewing, seems only to have come to a head to be summarily crushed, and the result is that Theognis has to retire into exile in Eubœa, Thebes, and Syracuse in succession. How he maintained himself in these places of refuge, turning his talents to account, and holding pretty staunchly to his principles, until a seasonable aid to the popular cause at the last-named sojourn, and a still more

seasonable *douceur* to the Corinthian general, paved
the way to his recall to Megara, will be seen in the
account we propose to give of the last epoch of his life,
which is supposed to have lasted till beyond 480 B.C.,
as he distinctly in two places refers to the instant terror of a Median invasion. That life divides itself into
the periods of his youth and prosperous estate, his
clouded fortunes at home, and his long and wearisome
exile. The remainder of this chapter will serve for a
glance at the first period.

That our poet was of noble birth may be inferred
from the confidence with which, in reply to an indignity put upon him in his exile at Thebes, to which
we shall refer in due course, he asserts his descent
from "noble Æthon," as if the very mention of the
name would prove his rank to his contemporaries; and
in the first fragment (according to the ingenious
chronological arrangement of Frere, which we follow
throughout), Theognis is found in the heyday of prosperity, praying Zeus, and Apollo, the special patron
of his fatherland, to preserve his youth

"Free from all evil, happy with his wealth,
In joyous easy years of peace and health."

Interpreting this language by its context, we learn
that his ideal of joyous years was to frequent the banquets of his own class, and take his part in songs
accompanied by the flute or lyre,—

"To revel with the pipe, to chant and sing —
This also is a most delightful thing.
Give me but ease and pleasure! what care I
For reputation or for property?"— (F.)

But we are not to suppose that such language as the last couplet wore so much the expression of his serious moods as of a gaiety rendered reckless by potations such as, we are obliged to confess, lent a not infrequent inspiration to his poetry. Theognis is, according to his own theory, quite *en règle* when he retires from a banquet

"Not absolutely drunk nor sober quite."

He glories in a state which he expresses by a Greek word, which seems to mean that of being fortified or steeled with wine, an ironical arming against the cares of life to which he saw no shame in resorting. And perhaps too implicit credence is not to be given to the professions of indifference to wealth and character which are made by a poet who can realise in verse such an experience as is portrayed in the fragment we are about to cite:—

"My brain grows dizzy, whirled and overthrown
  With wine: my senses are no more my own.
  The ceiling and the walls are wheeling round !*
  But let me try! perhaps my feet are sound.
  Let me retire with my remaining sense,
  For fear of idle language and offence."—(F.)

In his more sober moments the poet could appreciate

* Juvenal, in Satire vi. 477-479, describes drinking-bouts in imperial Rome prolonged—

"Till round and round the dizzy chambers roll,
  Till double lamps upon the table blaze,
  And stupor blinds the undiscerning gaze."
—Hodgson, 107.

pursuits more congenial to his vocation and intellectual cultivation, as is seen in his apparently early thirst for knowledge, and discovery that such thirst does not admit of thorough satisfaction:—

> "Learning and wealth the wise and wealthy find
> Inadequate to satisfy the mind—
> A craving eagerness remains behind;
> Something is left for which we cannot rest,
> And the last something always seems the best—
> Something unknown, or something unpossest."—(F.)

One who could give vent to such a sentiment may be supposed to have laid up in youth a store of the best learning attainable; and the bent of his talents, which was towards vocal and instrumental music and composition of elegies, was so successfully followed that in time of need he was able to turn it to means of subsistence. Indeed, that he knew what was really the real secret of success in a concert or a feast is seen in a remark which he addressed to a certain Simonides (whom there is no reason to identify with the famous poet), recommending

> "Inoffensive, easy merriment,
> Like a good concert, keeping time and measure;
> Such entertainments give the truest pleasure."—(F.)

But if the poet was able to preserve the health which he besought the gods to grant him, in spite of what we should call hard living, there are hints in his poetry that the "peace" which he coupled with it did not bless him uninterruptedly. In one of his earlier elegiac fragments there is a hint of a youthful passion,

broken off by him in bitterness at the Megarian flirt's
"love for every one." Such, at least, seems to be the
interpretation of four lines which may be closely rendered,—

> "While only I quaffed yonder secret spring,
> 'Twas clear and sweet to my imagining.
> 'Tis turbid now. Of it no more I drink,
> But hang o'er other stream or river-brink."—(D.)

He was determined, it seems, to be more discursive in
his admiration for the future. How that plan succeeded does not appear, though in several passages he
arrogates to himself a degree of experience as regards
women, and match-making, and the like. In the end
we have his word for it, that he proved his own
maxim,—

> "Of all good things in human life,
> Nothing can equal goodness in a wife."—(F.)

But this could not have been till long after he had
suffered rejection of his suit for a damsel whose
parents preferred a worse man—*i.e.*, a plebeian—and
had carried on secret relations with her after her
"mating to a clown." His own account of this is
curious, as its opening shows that he vented his
chagrin on himself:—

> "Wine I forswear, since at my darling's side
> A meaner man has bought the right to bide.
> Poor cheer for me! To sate her parents' thirst
> She seeks the well, and sure her heart will burst
> In weeping for my love and lot accurst.
> I meet her, clasp her neck, her lips I kiss,
> And they responsive gently murmur this:

'A fair but luckless girl, my lot has been
To wed perforce the meanest of the mean.
Oft have I longed to burst the reins, and flee
From hateful yoke to freedom, love, and thee."

Perhaps, on the whole, he had no great reason to speak well of the sex, for in one place, as if he looked upon marriage, like friendship, as a lottery, he moralises to the effect—

" That men's and women's hearts you cannot try
Beforehand, like the cattle which you buy;
Nor human wit and wisdom, when you treat
For such a purchase, can escape deceit:
Fancy betrays us, and assists the cheat."—(F.)

But, if his witness is true, mercenary parents were as common of old as in our own day. He was led, both by his exclusiveness as an aristocrat, and his impatience of a mere money-standard of worth, to a disgust of—

" The daily marriages we make,
Where price is everything: for money's sake
Men marry ; women are in marriage given.
The churl or ruffian that in wealth has thriven
May match his offspring with the proudest race ;
Thus everything is mixt, noble and base !"—(F.)

And that he did ponder the regeneration of society, and strive to fathom the depths of the education question agitated in the old world, we know from a passage in his elegies, which, though we have no clue to the time he wrote it, deserves to be given in this place, both as connected with his notions about birth, and as a set-off to the passages which have led us to picture him as more or less of an easy liver :—

> "To rear a child is easy, but to teach
> Morals and manners is beyond our reach;
> To make the foolish wise, the wicked good,
> That science yet was never understood.
> The sons of Esculapius, if their art
> Could remedy a perverse and wicked heart,
> Might earn enormous wages! But in fact
> The mind is not compounded and compact
> Of precept and example; human art
> In human nature has no share or part.
> Hatred of vice, the fear of shame and sin,
> Are things of native growth, not grafted in;
> Else wives and worthy parents might correct
> In children's hearts each error and defect:
> Whereas we see them disappointed still,
> No scheme nor artifice of human skill
> Can rectify the passions or the will."—(F.)

Not often, however, despite his sententiousness, which has been the cause of his metamorphose by posterity into a coiner of maxims for the use of schools and the instruction of life and morals, does Theognis muse in such a strain of seriousness. Oftener far his vein is bright and gay, as when he makes ready for a feast, which, if we are not mistaken, was destined to take most of the remainder of his "solid day."

> "Now that in mid career, checking his force,
> The bright sun pauses in his pride and force,
> Let us prepare to dine; and eat and drink
> The best of everything that heart can think;

And let the shapely Spartan damsel fair }
Bring with a rounded arm and graceful air }
Water to wash, and garlands for our hair: }
In spite of all the systems and the rules
Invented and observed by sickly fools,
Let us be brave, and resolutely drink ;
Not minding if the Dog-star rise or sink."—(F.)

A very pretty vignette might be made of this, or of a kindred fragment that seems to belong to his later days. And to tell the truth, the poet's rule seems to have been that you should "live while you may." Whether, as has been surmised by Mr Frere, he refers to the catastrophe of Hipparchus or not, the four lines which follow indicate Theognis's conviction that everything is fated,—a conviction very conducive to enjoyment of the passing hour. 'Let us eat and drink, for to-morrow we die ' :—

"No costly sacrifice nor offerings given
Can change the purpose of the powers of Heaven ;
Whatever Fate ordains, danger or hurt,
Or death predestined, nothing can avert."—(F.)

This conviction, no doubt, to a great degree influenced the poet's indifference to the honours of a pompous funeral, for which, considering his birth and traditions, he might have cherished a weakness. But his tone of mind, we see, was such that he could anticipate no satisfaction from "hat-bands and scarves," or whatever else in his day represented handsome obsequies. When some great chief, perhaps a tyrant, perhaps one of the heads of his party at Megara, was to be borne to his long home with a solemn pageant, Theognis has no mind to take a part in it, and expresses his reasons in language wherein the Epicurean vein is no less conspicuous than the touching common-sense :—

> "I envy not these sumptuous obsequies,
> The stately car, the purple canopies ;
> Much better pleased am I, remaining here,
> With cheaper equipage, and better cheer,
> A couch of thorns, or an embroidered bed,
> Are matters of indifference to the dead."—(F.)

This old-world expression of the common-place that the grave levels all distinctions is not unlike, save that it lacks the similitude of life to a river, the stanzas on "Man's Life," by a Spanish poet, Don Jorge Manrique, translated by Longfellow :—

> "Our lives are rivers, gliding free
> To that unfathomed boundless sea,
> The silent grave !
> Thither all earthy pomp and boast
> Roll to be swallowed up and lost
> In one dark wave.
>
> Thither the mighty torrents stray:
> Thither the brook pursues its way ;
> And tinkling rill.
> There all are equal : side by side,
> The poor man and the son of pride
> Lie calm and still."

But before Theognis could give proof of this levelling change, he had a stormy career to fulfil, as we shall find in the next chapter.

CHAPTER II.

THEOGNIS IN OPPOSITION.

From the indistinctness of our knowledge as to the sequence of events in Megara, it is impossible to fix the point of time when Theognis began to be a political plotter; but as, during the whole of his mature life, his party was in opposition, it will be enough to trace the adverse influence of the dominant democracy upon his career till it terminated in exile. We have seen that he was a member of a club composed of exclusive and aristocratic members, meeting ostensibly for feasting and good-fellowship, but really, as their designation "the good"—in a sense already explained—clearly indicated, designed and pledged to cherish the traditions of a constitution to which they were devoted, and which for the time being was suffering eclipse.

Of this club a certain Simonides was president, one Onomacritus a boon companion, and Cyrnus, to whom are addressed some two-thirds of the extant verses of Theognis, a younger member, of whom, politically, the greatest things were expected. Though its soirees seem

to have been often noisy and Bacchanalian, we must
suppose the Aristocratic Club at Megara to have been
as busy in contemporary politics as the "Carlton"
or the "Reform" in our general elections; and there
are tokens that Theognis was a sleepless member of
the Committee, although some of his *confrères*, of whom
little more than the names survive, cared more for
club-life than club-politics. There was one notable
exception. In spite of the waywardness of youth,
and the fickleness characteristic of one so petted and
caressed by his friends, Cyrnus must have lent his
ears and hands to various schemes of Theognis for up-
setting the democracy, and restoring the ascendancy of
the "wise and good." At times it is plain that Cyrnus
considered himself to have a ground of offence against
Theognis; and there are verses of the latter which
bespeak recrimination and open rupture, though of
course the poet compares himself to unalloyed gold,
and considers his good faith stainless. The elder of
the pair was probably tetchy and jealous, the younger
changeable and volatile; but there is certainly no
reason for supposing that Cyrnus's transference of his
friendship to some other political chief resulted in either
party-success or increase of personal distinction, for his
name survives only in the elegiacs of Theognis, as
indeed that poet has prophesied it would, in a fragment the key to which Hookham Frere finds in a comparison of bardic celebration with the glory resulting
from an Olympic victory:—

"You soar aloft, and over land and wave
Are borne triumphant on the wings I gave,

(The swift and mighty wings, Music and Verse).
Your name in easy numbers smooth and terse
Is wafted o'er the world ; and heard among
The banquetings and feasts, chaunted and sung,
Heard and admired ; the modulated air
Of flutes, and voices of the young and fair
Recite it, and to future times shall tell ;
When, closed within the dark sepulchral cell,
Your form shall moulder, and your empty ghost
Wander along the dreary Stygian coast.
  Yet shall your memory flourish green and young,
Recorded and revived on every tongue,
In continents and islands, every place
That owns the language of the Grecian race.
  No purchased prowess of a racing steed,
But the triumphant Muse, with airy speed,
Shall bear it wide and far, o'er land and main,
A glorious and imperishable strain ;
A mighty prize gratuitously won,
Fixed as the earth, immortal as the sun."—(F.)

  But, to catch the thread of Theognis's story, we must go back to earlier verses than these, addressed to the young noble whom he regarded with a pure and almost paternal regard—the growth, it may be, in the first instance of kindred political views. The verses of Theognis which refer to the second period of his life begin with a caution to Cyrnus to keep his strains as much a secret as the fame of his poetry will allow, and evince the same sensitiveness to public opinion as so many other of his remains. He cannot gain and keep, he regrets to own, the goodwill of his fellow-citizens, any more than Zeus can please all parties, whilst—

"Some call for rainy weather, some for dry."

What the advice was which required such a seal of secrecy begins to appear shortly, in a fragment which presages a revolution, in which Cyrnus is looked-to to play a leader's part. It is interesting as a picture of the state of things which one revolution had brought about, and for which Theognis was hatching a panacea in another. Slightly altered, to meet the political sense of the "good" and "bad," the "better-most" and the "worse" in Megarian parlance, the following extract from Mr Frere is a faithful transcript:—

"Our commonwealth preserves its former frame,
Our common people are no more the same;
They that in skins and hides were rudely dressed,
Nor dreamed of law, nor sought to be redressed
By rules of right, but, in the days of old,
Without the walls, like deer, their place did hold,
Are now *the dominant class,* and we, the rest,
Their betters nominally, once the best,
Degenerate, debased, timid, and mean;
Who can endure to witness such a scene?
Their easy courtesies, the ready smile
Prompt to deride, to flatter, to beguile!
Their utter disregard of right or wrong,
Of truth or honour! Out of such a throng
Never imagine you can choose a just
Or steady friend, or faithful to his trust.
  But change your habits! let them go their way!
Be condescending, affable, and gay!
Adopt with every man the style and tone,
Most courteous, most congenial with his own!
But in your secret counsels keep aloof
From feeble paltry souls, that at the proof

Of danger and distress are sure to fail,
For whose salvation nothing can avail."—(F.)

The last lines assuredly betoken the brewing of a conspiracy; but the poet goes on to lament a state of things where a generation of spiritless nobles replaces an ancestry remarkable for spirit and magnanimity. Though a government by an aristocracy of caste, if of this latter calibre, could not be upset, he has evident misgivings in reference to the present leaders of the party, whose pride he likens to that which ruined the centaurs, destroyed "Smyrna the rich and Colophon the great," and made "Magnesian ills"—in reference to the punishment of the oppressive pride of the Magnesians by the Ephesians at the river Mæanler—a by-word and a proverb in the verse of Archilochus, as well as of Theognis. In such a posture of affairs our poet professes an intention to hold aloof from pronounced politics and party—

"Not leaguing with the discontented crew,
Nor with the proud and arbitrary few :"—(F.)

just as elsewhere he advises Cyrnus to do, in a couplet which may be translated—

"Fret not, if strife the townsmen reckless make,
But 'twixt both sides, as I, the mid-way take."—(D.)

He was old enough to foresee the danger of reprisals, and, from policy, counselled younger blood to abstain from injustice and rapine, when the tide turned,—

"Cyrnus, proceed like me! walk not awry!
Nor trample on the bounds of property."—(F.)

but he soon found that his neutrality only procured
him the hatred and abuse of both friends and foes;
a discovery which he expresses thus:—

"The city's mind I cannot comprehend—
Do well or ill, they hold me not their friend.
From base and noble blame is still my fate,
Though fools may blame, who cannot imitate."—(D.)

It was hard, he thought, that his friends should look
coolly upon him, if, with a view to the wellbeing of
his party, he gave no offence to the opposite faction,—
if, as he puts it,

"I cross not my foe's path, but keep as clear,
As of hid rocks at sea the pilots steer."—(D.)

And he is almost querulous in his sensibility to public
opinion, when he sings,—

"The generous and brave in common fame
From time to time encounter praise or blame:
The vulgar pass unheeded: none escape
Scandal or insult in some form or shape.
Most fortunate are those, alive or dead,
Of whom the least is thought, the least is said."—(F.)

It is as if he administered to himself the comfort
which Adam gives Orlando—

"Know you not, master, to some kind of men
Their graces serve them but as enemies?
No more do yours; your virtues, gentle master,
Are sanctified and holy traitors to you."
—'As you like it,' II. iii.

But a candid study of the character of Theognis in-
duces the impression that his neutrality was only fit-

ful or temporary. A great deal of his counsel to his
friend exhibits him in the light of a politic watcher of
events, at one time deprecating what at another he
advocated. Who would recognise the champion of
the "wise and good" and of their policy, pure and
simple, in these verses, breathing a spirit of progress
and expediency?—

> "Waste not your efforts: struggle not, my friend,
> Idle and old abuses to defend.
> Take heed! the very measures that you press,
> May bring repentance with their own success."—(F.)

There is also an inconsistency to be accounted for
doubtless upon politic grounds, in the discrepant advice
which he gives Cyrnus as to the friend to be chosen
in the crisis then imminent. At one time he is all
for "determined hearty partisans," and deprecates association
with reckless associates, as well as with fair-
weather friends:—

> "Never engage with a poltroon or craven,
> Avoid him, Cyrnus, as a treacherous haven.
> Those friends and hearty comrades, as you think,
> Ready to join you, when you feast or drink,
> Those easy friends from difficulty shrink."—(F.)

But anon he is found subscribing to the principle that
"no man is wholly bad or wholly good," and recommending his friend to conciliate, as we say, Tom, Dick, and
Harry, so as to be "all things to all men."

> "Join with the world; adopt with every man
> His party views, his temper, and his plan;

> Strive to avoid offence, study to please
> Like the sagacious inmate of the seas,*
> That an accommodating colour brings,
> Conforming to the rock to which he clings:
> With every change of place changing his hue;
> The model for a statesman such as you."—(F.)

Perhaps the clue to this riddle is, that circumstances about this time drove Theognis into a more pronounced course,—as men get desperate when they lose those possessions which, whilst intact, justify them in being choice, and conservative, and exclusive. Either in a fresh political revolution and a new partition of the lands of the republic, or, as Mr Grote thinks, in a movement in favour of a single-headed despot accomplished by some of Theognis's own party, who were sick of the rule of the "bad rich," he lost his estate whilst absent on an unfortunate voyage. Thenceforth he is a conspirator at work to recover his confiscated lands by a counter-revolution: thenceforth his verses are a mixture of schemes for revenge, of murmurs against Providence, and of suspicion of the comrades whose partisanship he hoped might yet reinstate the old possessors of property. The two or three fragments which refer more or less directly to this loss may be given together. Here is one which speaks to the extent and nature of it:—

> "Bad faith has ruined me: distrust alone
> Has saved a remnant: all the rest is gone

---

* The creature referred to is the Sea-Polypus — *Sepia Octopodia* of Linnaeus — which is referred to in Hesiod's 'Works and Days' (524) under the epithet of "the boneless."

To ruin and the dogs : the powers divine
I murmur not against them, nor repine :
Mere human violence, rapine, and stealth
Have brought me down to poverty from wealth."—(F.)

In another he invokes the help of Zeus in requiting his friends and foes according to their deserts, whilst he describes himself as one who—

" Like to a scared and hunted hound
That scarce escaping, trembling and half drowned,
Crosses a gully, swelled with wintry rain,
Has crept ashore in feebleness and pain."—(F.)

The bitterness of his feelings at the wrong he has suffered is intensified, in the sequel of this fragment, into the expression of a wish "one day to drink the very blood" of them that have done it. But perhaps the most touching and specific allusion to his spoliation is where the return of spring—to send another's plough over his ancestral fields—brings up to his remembrance the change in his fortunes :—

" The yearly summons of the creaking crane,
That warns the ploughman to his task again,
Strikes to my heart a melancholy strain—
When all is lost, and my paternal lands
Are tilled for other lords with other hands,
Since that disastrous wretched voyage brought
Riches and lands and everything to nought."—(F.)

A kindred feeling of pain breathes in another passage à *propos* of autumn and its harvest-homes. And this pain he seeks to allay sometimes by reminding himself that womanish repinings will but gratify his foes, and at other times by plans for setting Providence to rights. Now he admits that patience is the only cure, and that, if impatient,—

> "We strive like children, and the Almighty plan
> Controls the froward, weak children of man."

Now again, he seems to think sullen resistance is a better policy; and in another curious musing he argues against the justice of visiting the sins of the fathers on the children:—

> "The case is hard where a good citizen,
> A person of an honourable mind,
> Religiously devout, faithful, and kind,
> Is doomed to pay the lamentable score
> Of guilt accumulated long before.
> . . . .
> Quite undeservedly doomed to atone,
> In other times, for actions not his own."—(F.)

In the midst of these conflicting emotions it is pleasant to find that he can extend a welcome out of the remnant of his fortunes to such hereditary friends as one Clearistus, who has come across the sea to visit him; and it is consistent with his early habits that he should try the effect of drowning care in the bowl, though he is forced to admit that this factitious oblivion soon gives place to bitter retrospects, and equally bitter prospects.

We must not however suppose that Theognis and his fellow-sufferers brooded altogether passively over their wrongs. His famous political verses, likening the state to a ship in a storm, betray a weakness in the

ruling powers, eminently provocative of the *émeute* or
insurrection which was to follow:—

> "Such is our state! in a tempestuous sea,
> With all the crew raging in mutiny!
> No duty followed, none to reef a sail,
> To work the vessel, or to pump or bale:
> All is abandoned, and without a check
> The mighty sea comes sweeping o'er the deck.
> Our steersman, hitherto so bold and steady,
> Active and able, is deposed already.
> No discipline, no sense of order felt,
> The daily messes are unduly dealt.
> The goods are plundered, those that ought to keep
> Strict watch are idly skulking, or asleep;
> All that is left of order or command
> Committed wholly to the basest hand.
> In such a case, my friend, I needs must think
> It were no marvel though the vessel sink.
> This riddle to my worthy friends I tell,
> But a shrewd knave will understand it well!"—(F.)

It is easy to discern in the last couplet a hint to his
partisans to take advantage of this posture of affairs,
and the fragments which serve as a context revert to
the drowning state, discuss who is staunch and what
is rotten in it, and imply generally that the sole reason
for not striking is distrust of the number and fitness
of the tools:—

> "The largest company you could enroll,
> A single vessel could embark the whole!
> So few there are: the noble manly minds,
> Faithful and firm, the men that honour binds;
> Impregnable to danger and to pain
> And low seduction in the shape of gain."—(F.)

But the time comes when such a chosen few have to be
resorted to, as a last resource, in preference to the ruin
certain to overtake them if, after their plots have been
divulged, they sit still and await it. There is extant
a passage of some length, which Mr Frere ingeniously
conceives to have been the heads of Theognis's speech
to the conspirators. Its conclusion represents the
oath of the malcontents, a formula pledging assistance
to friends and requital to foes to the very uttermost.
It breathes the courage of desperation, but does not
hold out a prospect of success which could justify
the resort to action. The precise nature of what followed
we know not. An elegiac and subjective poet
like Theognis is readier to moralise than to describe.
The outbreak may have had a gleam of success, or
may have been crushed at the beginning by the foresight
of its opponents, or the despair and faint heart of
its promoters. It seems quite clear, however, that,
perhaps by the aid of an armed force from some democratic
state, most likely Corinth, the insurrection is
beaten to its last breathing-place. Here is a fragment
which vividly pictures the hurried resolve of the party
of Cyrnus and Theognis to abandon their country and
ill-starred enterprise:—

" A speechless messenger, the beacon's light,
Announces danger from the mountain's height!
Bridle your horses and prepare to fly;
The final crisis of our fate is nigh.
A momentary pause, a narrow space,
Detains them: but the foes approach apace!

We must abide what fortune has decreed,
And hope that Heaven will help us at our need.
Make your resolve! At home your means were great;
Abroad you will retain a poor estate;
Unostentatious, indigent, and scant,
Yet live secure, at least from present want."—(F.)

Such, then, was the issue of all our poet's plotting and club-intrigues, his poetic exhortations, and his hopes of a saviour in Cyrnus. Not only did he fail of the aggrandisement of his party and the recovery of his estate: he had henceforth also to realise the miseries of exile.

CHAPTER III.

THEOGNIS IN EXILE.

DRIVEN from his country through an unsuccessful rising against the party in power, Theognis next appears as a refugee in Eubœa, where a faction of congenial political views has tempted him to take up his residence. But his sojourn must have been brief. The aristocracy of the island was no match for the commonalty, when the latter was backed by Corinthian sympathisers, whose policy was to upset hereditary oligarchies, and to lift an individual to supreme power on the shoulders of the people. Before this strong and sinister influence our poet probably had to bow in Eubœa, as he had already bowed in Megara. The principles to which he clung so tenaciously were doomed to ill luck, and he felt the disasters of his party little short of a personal disgrace. It was the old story of the *good* and *bad*, in the political and social sense already noticed; and, as at Megara, the good got the worst of it:—

"Alas for our disgrace! Cerinthus lost,[*]
The fair Lelantian plain! A plundering host

---

[*] Cerinthus was a city of Eubœa, and Lelantum a well-watered plain, which was an old source of contention betwixt the Eretrians and Chalcidians.

Invade it—all the *brave* banished or fled!
Within the town *lewd ruffians* in their stead
Rule it at random. Such is our disgrace.
May Zeus confound the Cypselising race!"—(F.)

Breathing from his heart this curse against the policy of the Corinthians above referred to, and conveniently named after the usurper who founded the system, Theognis soon retired to Thebes, as a state which, from its open sympathy with the politics of the banished Megarians, would be likeliest to offer them an asylum, and to connive at their projects for recovering their native city by force or subtlety. The first glimpse we have of him at Thebes is characteristic of the man in more ways than one. At the house of a noble host, his love of music led him to an interference with, or a rivalry of, the hired music-girl Argyris and her vocation, which provoked the gibes of the glee-maiden, and possibly lowered him in the estimation of the company. But the love of music and song, which led him into the scrape, sufficed also to furnish him with a ready and extemporised retort to the girl's insinuation that perhaps his mother was a flute-player (and, by implication, a slave)—a retort which he, no doubt, astonished his audience by singing to his own accompaniment:—

> "I am of Æthon's lineage. Thebes has given
> Shelter to one from home and country driven.
> A truce to jests: my parents mock thou not,
> For thine, not mine, girl, is the slavish lot.
> Full many an ill the exile has to brave :
> This good I clasp, that none can call me slave,

Or bought with price. A franchise I retain,
Albeit in dreamland, and oblivion's plain."—(D.)

The verses seem to be instinct with a *hauteur* bred from consciousness of his aristocratic connections, even whilst the singer's dependence upon his own talents rather than on hired minstrelsy bespeaks him a citizen of the world. But, apart from such scenes and such entertainments in hospitable Thebes, our poet found time there for schemes of revenge and reprisals, and for the refugee's proverbial solace, the pleasures of hope. Whilst a portion of his day was spent in the congenial society of the cultivated noble -- the *contretemps* at whose house does not seem to have interrupted their friendship—another portion was devoted to projects of return, which a fellow-feeling would prevent from appearing tedious to the ear of his partner in exile, Cyrnus. To him it is amusing to find him comparing his hardships to those of Ulysses, and gathering hope of vengeance from the sequel of the wanderings of that mythical hero :—

" Doomed to descend to Pluto's dreary reign,
Yet he returned and viewed his home again,
And wreaked his vengeance on the plundering crew,
The factious, haughty suitors, whom he slew:
Whilst all the while, with steady faith unfeigned,
The prudent, chaste Penelope remained
With her fair son, waiting a future hour
For his arrival and return to power."—(F.)

According, indeed, to Theognis's testimony, it should seem that his Penelope at Megara was as blameless as

the Ithacan princess of that name, for he takes Cyrnus
to witness, in a quaint fashion enough, that

> "Of all good things in human life,
> Nothing can equal goodness in a wife.
> In our own case we prove the proverb true;
> You vouch for me, my friend, and I for you."—(F.)

It must be allowed that this is a confirmation, under
the circumstances, of the poet's dictum, "that absence
is not death to those that love;" but still one is
tempted to wonder what their wives at Megara thought
of these restless, revolution-mongering husbands, as
they beheld them in the mind's eye hobbing and nob-
bing over treason in some "Leicester Square" tavern
of Eubœa or of Thebes. In such *tête-à-têtes* Theognis,
no doubt, was great in æsthetics as well as moralities;
and the sole deity still left to reverence, Hope, became
more winsome to his fancy as he dwelt on the refinements he had to forego, now that he was bereft of
home and property. The following fragment represents this state of feeling:—

> "For human nature Hope remains alone
> Of all the deities—the rest are flown.
> Faith is departed; Truth and Honour dead;
> And all the *Graces* too, my friend, are fled.
> The scanty specimens of living worth
> Dwindled to nothing and extinct on earth.
> Yet while I live and view the light of heaven
> (Since Hope remains, and never hath been driven
> From the distracted world) the single scope
> Of my devotion is to worship Hope:
> Where hecatombs are slain, and altars burn,
> With all the deities adored in turn,

Let Hope be present: and with Hope, my friend,
Let every sacrifice commence and end."—(F.)

Mr Frere notes the characteristic touch in the fourth line, "The victim of a popular revolution lamenting that democracy has destroyed the Graces." But as time passed, and the exiles still failed to compass their return, distrust and impatience begin to be rife amongst them. Theognis applies the crucible, which frequently figures in his poetry, and might almost indicate a quondam connection with the Megarian Mint, and fails to discover a sterling unadulterated mind in the whole range of his friends. In bitterness of spirit he finds out at last that

" An exile has no friends! no partisan
Is firm or faithful to the banished man;
A disappointment and a punishment
Harder to bear and worse than banishment."—(F.)

And under these circumstances he is driven in earnest to the course which, in his 'Acharnians,' Aristophanes represents Dicaeopolis as adopting—namely, private negotiations with the masters of the situation at Megara. Ever recurring to his "pleasant gift of verse" when he had "a mot" to deliver, a shaft of wit to barb, or a compliment to pay, Theognis makes it the instrument wherewith to pave the way to his reconciliation and restoration. If the whole poems were extant, of which the lines we are about to cite represent Frere's mode of translating the first couplet, it would, as the translator acutely surmises, be found to contain a candid review of the past, an admission of errors on his own side, an

advance towards making things pleasant with the
other, and a first overture to the treaty he was desirous to negotiate with the victorious party.

> "No mean or coward heart will I commend
> In an old comrade or a party friend;
> Nor with ungenerous hasty zeal decry
> A noble-minded gallant enemy."—(F.)

But the bait, though specious, did not tempt those
for whom it was designed. In another short fragment
is recorded the outburst of the poet's disappointment
at finding it "labour lost." He seems to have abandoned hope at last in the words—

> "Not to be born—never to see the sun -
> No worldly blessing is a greater one!
> And the next best is speedily to die,
> And lapt beneath a load of earth to lie."—(F.)

But even a man without hope must live—that is,
unless he terminate his woes by self-slaughter, a *dernier ressort* to which, to do him justice, Theognis makes
no allusion. And so—it would seem because Thebes,
though it gave sympathy and hospitality, did not give
means of earning a subsistence to the Megarian refugees—we find him in the next fragment—the last
of those addressed to Cyrnus—announcing a resolution to flee from poverty, the worst of miseries:—

> "In poverty, dear Cyrnus, we forego
> Freedom in word and deed—body and mind,
> Action and thought are fettered and confined.
> Let us then fly, dear Cyrnus, once again!
> Wide as the limits of the land and main,

From these entanglements ; with these in view,
Death is the lighter evil of the two."—(F.)

Possibly, as we hear no more of him, the poet's younger and less sensitive comrade did not respond to the invitation. Certainly Theognis shortly transferred his residence to Sicily, that isle of the west, which was to his countrymen what America is to ours, the refuge of unemployed enterprise and unappreciated talent. Arrived there, he quickly shakes off the gloom which the impressions of a sea-voyage would not tend to lighten, and prepares to grapple in earnest the problem " how to manage to live." Though he gives vent to expressions which show what an indignity work must have seemed to

" A manly form, an elevated mind,
   Once elegantly fashioned and refined,"

his pluck and good sense come to his aid, and he consoles himself with the generalisation that

" All kinds of shabby shifts are understood,
   All kinds of art are practised, bad and good,
   All kinds of ways to gain a livelihood."—(F.)

Not that he descends in his own person to any unworthy art or part. Having satisfied himself that his voice and skill in music were his most marketable gifts, he set up as an assistant performer at musical festivals ; and, in one of his pieces, he apologises for his voice being likely to fail at one of those entertainments, because he had been out late the night before serenading for hire. The poor gentleman no doubt had to do dirty work, and to put up with snubs he never dreamed of in his palmy club-life at home. His sensibilities were outraged by vulgar *nouveaux riches* who employed his talent, as well as by professionals who quizzed him as an amateur. Fortunately he could get his revenge in a cheap way upon both classes. Here is his thrust at the former:—

"Dunces are often rich, while indigence
Thwarts the designs of elegance and sense.
Nor wealth alone, nor judgment can avail;
In either case art and improvement fail."—(F.)

As to the latter, nothing can be more fair and open than the test to which he proposes to submit his own pretensions, and those of one Academus, who had twitted him with being a cross between an artist and an amateur:—

"I wish that a fair trial were prepared,
Friend Academus! with the prize declared,
A comely slave, the conqueror's reward;
For a full proof betwixt myself and you,
Which is the better minstrel of the two.
Then would I show you that a *mule* surpasses
In his performance all the breed of *asses*.
Enough of such discourse: now let us try
To join our best endeavours, you and I,
With voice and music; since the Muse has blessed
Us both with her endowments; and possessed
With the fair science of harmonious sound
The neighbouring people, and the cities round."—(F.)

The retort was two-edged. Whilst Theognis turns

the laugh against an ungenerous rival, and this in the
spirit of a true gentleman, he finds a sly means of
paying a delicate compliment to the taste of the public,
upon whose appreciation of music he had to depend
for support. It is plain that he gauged that public accurately. By degrees it becomes evident that he is
getting on in his chosen profession—not indeed to the
extent of being able, as he puts it in a terse couplet,
"to indulge his spirit to the full in its taste for the
graceful and beautiful," but, at all events, of having
wherewithal to discourse critically on the question of
indulgence and economy, from which we infer that he
had made something to save or to lose. After weighing the *pros* and *cons* in a more than usually didactic
passage, he confides to his hearers and readers the
reason why he inclines to a moderate rather than a
reckless expenditure:—

> "For something should be left when life is fled
>   To purchase decent duty to the dead;
>   Those easy tears, the customary debt
>   Of kindly recollection and regret.
>   Besides, the saving of superfluous cost
>   Is a sure profit, never wholly lost;
>   Not altogether lost, though left behind,
>   Bequeathed in kindness to a friendly mind.
>   And for the present, can a lot be found
>   Fairer and happier than a name renowned,
>   And easy competence, with honour crowned;
>   The just approval of the good and wise,
>   Public applauses, friendly courtesies;
>   Where all combine a single name to grace

With honour and pre-eminence of place,
Coevals, elders, and the rising race?"—(F.)

With these laudable ambitions he pursued with profit his calling of "director of choral entertainments," until, it would seem, upon the incidence of a war between Hippocrates, the tyrant of Gela, and the Syracusans, he was induced to go out in the novel character of a champion of freedom to the battle of Helorus. When Corinth and Corcyra combined to deliver Syracuse from the siege which followed the loss of this battle, it is probable that the Corinthian deputies were surprised to find the poet, whom they had known as an oligarchist at Megara, transformed into a very passable democrat, and seeking their good offices, with regard to his restoration to his native city. These, however, he found could not be obtained except through a bribe ; and accordingly, whilst he no doubt complied with the terms, he could not resist giving vent to his disgust in a poem wherein the Corinthian commander is likened to Sisyphus, and which ends with the bitter words—

"Fame is a jest; favour is bought and sold;
No power on earth is like the power of gold."—(F.)

It should seem that the bribe did pass, and that while the negotiations consequent upon it were pending, Theognis drew so near his home as friendly Lacedæmon, where he composed a pretty and Epicurean strain that tells its own story :—

> "Enjoy your time, my soul! another race
> Will shortly fill the world, and take your place,
> With their own hopes and fears, sorrow and mirth :
> I shall be dust the while an l crumbled earth.
> But think not of it ! Drink the racy wine
> Of rich Taygetus, press'd from the vine
> Which Theotimus, in the sunny glen
> (Old Theotimus loved by gods and men),
> Planted and watered from a plenteous source,
> Teaching the wayward stream a better course :
> Drink it, and cheer your heart, and banish care :
> A *load* of wine will *lighten* your despair."—(F.)

When in the concluding fragments (we follow Mr Hookham Frere's arrangement here as in most instances) Theognis is found reinstated in his native country, the sting of politics has been evidently extracted, as a preliminary ; and the burden of his song thenceforth is the praise of wine and of banquets. These are his recipes, we learn in a passage which contributes to the ascertainment of his date, for driving far

> "All fears of Persia, and her threatened war,"—

an impending danger, to which he recurs vaguely in another passage. It has been surmised from his speaking of age and death as remote, and of convivial pleasures as the best antidote to the fear of these, that he was not of very advanced age at the battle of Marathon. It is to be hoped that, when restored to home after his long exile, his wife was alive to receive him with warmer welcome than his children, to whom

he alludes as ungrateful and undutiful. Probably they
had been estranged from him during his absence by
the influence of the party in power, and they may also
have been ill pleased at his devotion to the artistic
pursuits which ministered to his substance in exile
and loss of fortune. To the end of his days, peace-
ful it should seem and undisturbed thenceforward,
he fulfilled his destiny as a "servant of the Muses,"
recognising it as a duty to spread the fruit of his
poetic genius, rather than, as in his earlier years, to
limit it to his inner circle of friends and relatives :—

> "Not to reserve his talent for himself
> In secret, like a miser with his pelf."—(F.)

It would be unhandsome in us to take leave of
Theognis without a word of felicitation to the poet's
shade on the happy rehabilitation which he has met
with at the hands of modern scholars. Time was—a
time not so very long ago—when the comparatively
few who were acquainted with the remains of Theognis
saw in him simply a stringer together of maxims in
elegiac verse, such as Xenophon had accounted him ;
and Isocrates had set him down in the same category
with Hesiod and Phocylides. But, thanks to the Ger-
mans, Welcker and Müller, and to the scholarly English-
man, John Hookham Frere, the elegiac poet of Megara
has been proved to be something more than a compiler
of didactic copy-slips—a scholar, poet, and politician in
one, with a biography belonging to him, the threads of

which are not hard to gather up. The result is, not that his maxims are less notable, but that we realise the life and character of him who moulded them into verse—verse which is often elegant in expression, and always marked by a genuine and forcible subjectivity. The task of tracing this life in his works has been rendered easier to the author of the foregoing pages by the ingenious and skilful labours of Mr Frere.

END OF HESIOD AND THEOGNIS.

www.ingramcontent.com/pod-product-compliance
Lightning Source LLC
Chambersburg PA
CBHW020302170426
43202CB00008B/463